HANDBOOK of APPLIED LEADERSHIP in EDUCATION

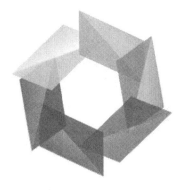

Dr Jacques Mostert

www.iale.org.za

INSTITUTE OF APPLIED LEADERSHIP IN EDUCATION PUBLICATIONS

Copyright © 2018 Jacques Mostert

Published by Institute of Applied Leadership in Education© in collaboration with International College of Leaders in Education ©.

20 Moore Street, Jansen Park, Boksburg, Gauteng, South Africa

Cover design by K Creative – Kobus Vermeulen
www.kcreative.co.za

ISBN-10: 1986754529
ISBN-13: 978-1986754521

For Grace

Dedicated to my parents, Judith and Johan, and my nephews Daniël and Lukas.

Thank you to Nandia, Simon, Bojan and Ibrahim for believing in me.

TABLE OF CONTENT

IV   72

INCLUSIVE EDUCATION   72

VI	**127**

MOTIVATION   127

ABOUT THE AUTHOR

With well over two decades of expertise gained in the global Education sector, Dr Jacques Mostert is an experienced and published education leader, researcher, professor, teacher, moderator, presenter and faculty coordinator.

An expert in the development and rollout of leadership training, curriculum development, multimedia tutorials and experiential learning techniques, Dr Mostert has dedicated his vocational passion for continuous improvement in classroom practice to the innovation of guidance and facilitation techniques and tools, and the production of peer training materials to transform leadership in education in step with the shift towards experiential knowledge acquisition, and increased dominance of technology-based learning among today's youth.

During his three-year tenure with the American University of the Middle East (AUM) in Kuwait most recently, Dr Mostert excelled in multi-disciplinary scholarly research outputs, while he gained invaluable practice as key member of the leadership corps of the Liberal Arts Department. As course moderator of Psychological Sciences (Human Motivation, Self-Development, Leadership, Academic Character and Skills Development) in the Liberal Arts Department, he worked in collaboration with faculties across the College of Business Administration.

Backed by more than two decades of diverse experience in secondary and further education and training (ranging from ages 11 to 18), through leadership and didactic practice that earned commendation from Her Majesty's Office for Standards in Education (Ofsted), Dr Mostert presents an impeccable academic and performance record, with expansive management, quality

i

control and commercial experience gained in the process. Highly engaged and energised to contribute to staff development via various seminars on current pedagogical practices, leadership and school improvement and more broadly, he also wrote, produced and directed several student plays, and musical revues.

His emerging research career has culminated in eight peer-reviewed articles published over less than three years, showcasing talent for assimilating existing and new knowledge across broad disciplines. This deep curiosity in culture, art and human engagement has placed Dr Mostert in diverse environments internationally, where he honed advanced change management abilities.

PREFACE

The general problem with writing a handbook of leadership in education lies not in determining and refining the audience, nor does it rest with establishing the need for such a book. The problem comes in when you think about practical issues such as convincing leaders that finding time to read and reflect, or providing functional theoretical and practical perspective to working school leaders that are knee-deep in the day-to-day business of raising standards and shaping lives. Many of the theoretical perspectives on leadership are abstract concepts and models that are far removed from authentic school systems.

There are several models that authors of leadership books may choose to follow. Many emphasise the personal qualities of leaders but provide little information on the authentic behaviours of leaders. Others emphasise theoretical models but don't spend much time at providing practical advice. Most authors of leadership books want to keep their audience as broad as possible by addressing general corporate perspectives infused with the newest pop-psychology trends such as the mindful leader or the top 8 habits of effective leaders. In the same way, not many leadership writers pay specific attention to leadership in education for myriad reasons including the fact not many school leaders will pick up the newest edition of leadership now in the airport bookstore.

Another problem with writing about leadership in education is that when school leaders find the time to read, and if they do find a book that is slanted towards their needs as school leaders, they tend to either affirm and follow the what is written, or they revert to what comes easy in the daily grind of the school mill. This leaves them without gaining the benefit of reflecting on their leadership behaviour and considering alternative strategies for enacting their leadership roles.

For these reasons and probably many more, the line I decided to follow in this book is called the functional approach. A functional approach or applied leadership as I have called it depends on the leader to know as much as, or more, about the school system and educational context that is being led as about the theoretical perspectives or personal qualities of the leaders. I have attempted to create a fusion of the theoretical and psychological aspects of leadership with the practical implementation of these constructs into the ten chapters of this book.

In the writing of each chapter, I have reflected on over two decades of my own experience in school improvement and leadership in education. I have reflected on what has worked and those failures that have shaped the way I look at schools and those that function within their walls. I have reflected on the reasons for why I have decided to write about leadership and not psychology, and the ultimate purpose of this book. This process has been intensely personal, and I did not shy away from exploring my shortcomings as teacher and leader of teachers, as I hope you will too. Nor have I shied away from recognising my strengths and building on those aspects that have served me well, as I hope you will also do.

The ultimate purpose of this book is to provide you with the information and support you need to become a masterful leader in your school, as well as a reference for you to affirm that the leadership behaviours and decisions you are making are purpose driven and valid. What you will not find between these pages are reams of anecdotes and tales of superhero mega leaders that have conquered the world. As leaders in education our everyday lives are filled with stories that would put Booker Prize Winning fiction writers to shame and the biographers of disgraced sport heroes reaching for their pens with incredulity. No I will not be padding these pages with filler stories. I sometimes wonder if such page padding is effective and if indeed readers ponder their applicability or merely glace over them to get to the intended punchline? For me, to be effective, an anecdote must be more powerful that the punch line. It must be self-evident and leave you the reader tossing and turning for nights on end before it is worth taking up your time and cutting down additional trees. Often, even the most seasoned of authors fall in the trap of over explaining and elaborating a point that could have been stated succinctly. Now that I have gotten that off my chest I want to jump right in and break the very rule I have just committed myself to by telling you a story I encountered on the opening pages of an airport edition self-help digest with exactly the type of conference openers as I spoke of above.

In the mid-1990s a party of eight seasoned mountaineers set out to ascend the final stage of Everest. They had the best equipment sponsors could buy, trained with veteran Everest climbers and their game plan had evidently been successful if judged by the close to mundane ascension so far. When you climb Everest, there are certain unwritten rules of which the most urgent is that after a specific time, you remain at camp and live to conquer the final slopes another day. However, the team of eight, confident that their plan has been fool proof and determined to stick to their schedule, decided to stay their course. By the time they reached Everest's summit, night had fallen and they were forced to descend in the dark. None survived.

The lesson learned from the unfortunate tale of determination and staying the course is that sometimes you must realise that no matter how well the plan you have been following has worked in the past, the time will always come to abandon the tested and set on a new path. The analogy, according to the author is that the world has changed. This we all know, but the problem is that despite the fact that the world has changed, the way we live and function in it has not. I want to extend his explanation and include education to this understanding. Education has been spoilt with a wealth of research and initiatives to bolster our understanding of the neurology and developmental psychology of learning. Ground-breaking methods in Teaching Learning and Assessment (TLA) and getting young people to learn abounds. Technology has made what once could only be imagined visual and in many cases tangible, the problem, however, is that, like our party of eight mountaineers, teachers and school leaders are holding on to the way things used to work, and believe so strongly that education was much more rigorous back in the day, that we are not seeing the danger of climbing Everest of education in the dark.

This book is about developing your capacity to lead, not in the way the titans of school corridors used to – with trepidation following in their wake. The purpose of this book is for you to develop your own sense of purpose, vision and personal signature as a leader. To climb your Everest in the bright sunlight. To be the change you want to see in the world.

I

Leadership Attribution Development

As part of your development and growth as a school leader, you should not only consider the skill with which you lead, the style that in which you share the common vision and your capacity to grow professionally. You should also set out on a path of attribution development.

When we think about who we are, our personalities and personal traits and attributions, we often believe that these aspects of ourselves are fixed. The truth is far from it, and like most things involving the human brain, plasticity plays a significant role. Recent research has proven that the brain's ability to adapt and adjust despite serious injury is close to miraculous. What we have previously thought to be impossible has now, through dedicated rehabilitation, become common practice. It has also become evident that adult brains, contrary to previous belief, do have the capacity to develop new neurons. However, the key words we should keep in mind are dedicated and rehabilitation. Both suggest an ongoing process of deliberate actions that force the brain to engage in changes, that over time, can heal and restore its capacity. With such proof, there is now little suggestion of an old dog not being able to learn new tricks. Why is this important? It is important to know that our ability to change the way we have done things, the way we have thought about things and the way we have taught others to do things does not wane, but remains an active aspect of human growth and development.

The remainder of this chapter, and this book, is based on your understanding that your brain is ready to accept new knowledge and from this new knowledge form new memories; that new memory, in turn, enables you to develop new skills and understanding; which in turn can lead to developing better habits, thus enabling you to become a masterful leader.

The attributes that are typical to you and your leadership style, which you will have to take under evaluation include emotional awareness and your capacity to manage emotions, growing your confidence and self-confidence (no they are not the same), developing and fostering trustworthiness, flexibility, developing and sustaining positive habits, nurturing empathy and your ability to resolve conflicts. We will be exploring each of these attributes as the foundation on which you will develop your leadership skills into mastery in the remaining chapters.

Leadership Values

There is a clear distinction between value and values, both of which play an important role in leadership growth and development. The first, value, refers to the actual worth in either financial or emotional terms you attach to an object, person or aspect of your life. When you look at why you are motivated to behave in a specific way, you will find you are more inclined to behave in ways that will result in outcomes that are valuable to you. This includes how you establish your vision for your school and the goals that you set for yourself as a leader as well as the goals you will set for the school.

The latter, your values, look more at those intangible aspects of your character and personality that has specific ethical or moral importance to you. These intangible aspects of who you are may include personality attributes such as humility and resilience. They may also include your ability to communicate, listen and have empathy for those you encounter. Most leaders have encountered the concept of a values clarification, a concept we will not spend much time on here. However, I want to make use of this opportunity to remind you that having a clear understanding of the values you hold, will not only provide you with the awareness of how and why you find certain aspects of leadership easier or more difficult than others. For example, if care and empathy are two important values that you hold dear to your heart, you may find it difficult to reprimand and punish teachers or support staff when such actions are called for. Whereas if diligence, punctuality and mastery are at the core of your values, you will find it relatively easy to hold teachers accountable for being tardy or lackadaisical in the completion of administrative duties.

3

Values that are most admire in leaders include humility, integrity, honesty, resilience, fairness, compassion, respect, responsibility, inspiration and the ability to learn. From this list, you may recognise some of the values that you ascribe to, and you may look at some of them and realise that you have not even considered them as necessary at all. You may feel a sense of dread that not one of your core values is listed here. Not to worry, remember these are values that others favour. They are not a list of values that are quintessential to being a leader. What is essential though is that you know what your values are and that it is evident that you are living those values in every aspect of your leadership life.

Therefore at the onset of this journey into your leadership mastery, I want you to take some time and consider which are the top five values you hold dearly and I want you to identify how you can demonstrate these values several times every day. This, however, is not enough, you must be sure that if at any point a stranger walks up to a teacher in your school and asks whether they can identify your values, it must be second nature for them to get at least the top three of them correct. It is worth spending some time on creating a "My Values" poster and put it on display outside your office, and every time you or anybody else walks into your office, there will be an expectation of encountering these values in the interactions and interpersonal relationships you develop between those walls. It is always a good idea to inculcate this habit across the entire school, from teachers to students, custodial and support staff all the way to parents and trustees.

Emotions

One of the most important attributes of any leader is the ability to have a clear awareness of their emotions and how their emotions influence their leadership behaviours and interpersonal relationships. Emotional control is only possible if you understand how emotions can drive, influence and impact on your behaviour and reactions. Emotions and behaviour are inextricably linked. You will be reminded of this fact throughout the remained of this book, and it is such an important point to remember that I will repeat the following paragraph, often verbatim, to ensure that none of its significance is lost between the lines.

Emotions are both the genesis as well as the consequence of behaviour; one cannot exist without the other. Experiencing emotions, being acutely aware of your emotions and effective leadership behaviours are not mutually exclusive. And those that suggest that complete objectivity and clinical rationality are preferable leadership attributes are missing out on the most powerful driving force of realising mastery in any field. Without going into the minutiae of the constituent aspects of emotions, we can look at how our feelings influence our behaviour in four ways. Emotions are either activating or deactivation, pleasant or unpleasant. Activating pleasant emotions (excitement, hap-piness, delight and anticipation) drive behaviour forward and if those emotions are enjoyable and pleasing, we tend to experience fulfilment in engaging in that behaviour. Unpleasant activating emotions (stress, anger, anxiety and fear) also drive behaviour but are less effective as motivators because there is only so much stress or anger a person can tolerate before burnout or inefficacy sets in. Deactivating emotions are barriers to action. They are pleasant (relaxed, content, satisfied, comfortable and pleased) and contribute to the recuperation of your emotional capital, or they are unpleasant (depressed, sad, fatigued and drained). Deactivating unpleasant emotions do not contribute to recuperation insofar as the cortisol loop, which drives our stress hormones is not deactivated, and we still experience the unpleasant strain of feeling bad.

It is important to know that emotions have a significant impact on your behaviour. In any specific situation, you experience your feelings first and only then do you react. Having an awareness of how you feel, why you feel that way, whether those feelings are activating or deactivating and by having an understanding of how you usually react when you experience those specific feelings, empowers you to take control of your emotions. And, if you can control your unpleasant activating emotions in such a way that they do not become a barrier to interpersonal relationships, and if you can utilise your activating emotions to drive your leadership behaviour, and use pleasant deactivating emotions to recharge, you will become a much better leader. Secondly, if you can recognise how emotions are directing the behaviours of your teachers and support staff and facilitate the development of emotional control, you will find that building interpersonal relationship is much more comfortable and more sustainable than without it.

Fear

Before we look at a strategy that can help you develop emotional control, it is worth looking at both the benefits and barriers of fear. Fear, in my opinion, is what has kept our species at the crown of nature. It is because of the fear response that we have been able to sustain our evolution across the past hundred thousand or more years (depending on who you ask). It is also the cognitive inability of teenagers to recognise fear that has contributed to most of the adolescent deaths across the same time span. Therefore, I do not propagate that we should suppress our emotions of fear when we take on a new challenge or start a school improvement program. However, it is also important to recognise that fear can be a major impeding aspect of your leadership success. An acronym I wish to borrow from Stephen Gribben is Fear is Evidence Appearing to be Real. If we continually look at the evidence of every situation that makes us feel fear, and we do not contextualise that evidence, whether it appears to be real or not, we stand the chance of developing a sense of helplessness and desperation.

Fear can be debilitating or a call to action. Allow me to explain. The driving force of your emotions is found in a small but significant part of your brain called the amygdala. The amygdala is an integral part of the limbic system, which in turn regulates hormones, forms and recovers memories and, drives your emotions. The amygdala has a repertoire of three emotions, from which all of the various feelings you experience emanate: fear, anger and ease. The actions that are associated with these emotions are a fight, flight or no action at all. What is, however, more significant than the mere experience of these cognitive states, is the embodiment of these emotions. Right next to the amygdala are the hippocampus and the hypothalamus. From here the limbic system sends a torrent of the hormone cortisol to the adrenal glands, just above your kidneys, which in turn floods your body with adrenaline. It is this surge of adrenaline that makes us "feel" the emotions we do, and also what makes us react to the core emotions of fear, anger or ease. And it is precisely this feeling that lies at the core of emotional control.

Once you can recognise the deluge of adrenalin rush through to your heart and lungs, that is when your first thought should be stop, wait, control.

Developing Emotional Control

For you to develop emotional control, you can follow the following ABCD model, and like any skill, it will take repetition and considered practise to develop your skill of emotional control.

There are three As in the model: awareness of, assigning and accepting emotions. In every situation, you must practise becoming aware of how and what you feel. We often feel a blend of emotions, both pleasant and unpleasant, but one of those feelings will stand out, and that is the emotion you need to pay more attention to. Assigning a name to the emotion helps you understand why you are feeling the way you do. If you feel anxiety, it is possible for you to understand the reason for you are experiencing the emotion is that the possible outcome of the situation is important to you. The third A in our trilogy is acceptance. Firstly accepting that experiencing the emotion is valid and that there is no shame in experiencing it, and secondly, accepting that the situation causing the emotion has occurred and that feeling the emotions should serve as a vehicle for finding a solution rather than becoming deactivated.

The B in the model stands for breathing. The act of taking five deep breaths and exhaling slowly over seven counts each has a biological effect on the cortisol loop in your body. The increased oxygen in your blood allows the impact of adrenaline release to subside faster and returns control over your behaviour to the more measured front part of your brain (your prefrontal and orbitofrontal cortex) from the very reactive limbic system. Now that you have gained control over your biologic systems again, you can direct your frontal lobes to engage in the dual Cs of the control model.

You now can place the emotions you are feeling as well as the events that affected you in clear context. Why do you feel this way? What has happened in the past that has contributed to these feelings and how did you behave previously when you experienced these feelings? The context allows you to evaluate the benefits and barriers of reacting in specific ways and allows you to make better decisions in the situation. One of the most important aspects of emotional control is to challenge your assumptions. As humans, we are genetically predisposed to a self-serving bias that means we will as a rule of thumb assume that events of situations will revolve around our own interests. Ironically in most cases, events tend not to be personal or intentional. However, our self-serving bias makes us think that they are. Once you have had the chance to challenge your assumptions and see the wood from the trees, you come to the D in the model, the opportunity to decide what course of action would be most beneficial.

Imagine, on your way to an important meeting; you suddenly see the flow of the highway is slowing down and you end up getting stuck in traffic. At the onset frustration and anxiety becomes part of your already emotionally elevated experience. In most cases, frustration becomes the dominant emotion and you lash out at those other drivers that are in the same predicament as you. Now, imagine that you have been practising taking control of your emotions. You realise that you are feeling frustration and anxiety because the meeting you have to attend is crucial to you. You know that most of the stakeholders you are set to meet with knows that the road to the venue is notoriously unpredictable, however you don't want to assume that they will understand that traffic at that very point in time has come to a standstill, and because you know that being late will have a negative impression on them, you know you must take a course of action. Instead of lashing out and angrily pressing your car's horn, trying to force your way into the emergency lane, you make a call to the parties who you are scheduled to meet. Apologise for the inconvenience, and concentrate on driving safely. In this example you became aware of the emotions as you realise traffic is slowing down, you could name the emotion and understand why you are feeling it and through acceptance that there is nothing you could do, you managed to place the situation in context, avoid detrimental assumptions and could choose a course of action that could lead to a better outcome. Emotional control should become your number one leadership habit.

The Powerful Impact of Positive Habits

We often dedicate a significant amount of time to establishing standard operating procedures and managerial practices, yet we neglect the personal habits that help us become successful. Habits are behaviours that we repeatedly engage in without being prompted. If you have a checklist with daily *to do* behaviours on, those are not habits yet. To establish positive habits you have to consciously and deliberately engage in activities that will grow your leadership behaviours. In addition to the day-to-day behaviours that underline success, habits are also the safety net that will catch you when times get tough.

Nobody can expect that leadership is smooth sailing. Leadership is one of the career paths that carries with it a very high degree of uncertainty. And when the tough times come, the habits you have acquired along the way will predict how you behave. You will either respond reactively or proactively. To have a laissez-faire approach to developing habits leaves you vulnerable reactive responses, and if you have not managed to secure your ability to control your emotions well, such knee-jerk reactions will not serve you well. That is why it is important to deliberately focus on developing the type of habits that will contribute to success. Such habits include finding and celebrating the success of others; to continuously seek new experiences and new things to learn; to not try and force a work/life balance, but instead think "life"; to be empathetic and care for the well-being of others; to have something to prove to yourself; do not consider yourself as anything special and place emphasis on dignity and respect, rather than success. These habits should take the form of self-talk and reflection, become evident through your behaviour and your discussions with others.

Confidence

Controlled emotions and secure positive habits often manifest in the form of confidence – the face of knowing what we are doing and the ability to do it well, that we show to the rest of the world. A concise definition of confidence is that you are precise and secure in your worth, value, capability and potential with which you approach leading your school. However, we all know that every so often, notwithstanding your ability to control your sense of fear, your confidence fails you, and your amygdala conquers the mediating impact of your frontal lobes' ability to control your emotions. This is very normal, and helps us to understand and contextualise the situations we are facing. Confidence is external; we gain it over time through the outcomes, conversations, and reactions of others. Positive feedback results in a strong sense of confidence and negative feedback erode the confidence we may have. It is important to note that confidence is hardly ever a stable trait and that fluctuation depending on the situation and context is normal.

The other side of the confidence coin is not doubt or uncertainty, but rather self-confidence. The internal sense of certainty, aplomb and assurance of your ability, skill and capacity for leadership mastery. Self-confidence is based on your inner voice that that asserts the self-awareness of your ability to be a leader. Self-confidence is a highly personal and private world that you hardly ever reveal, and when you do, it usually is in the realm of coaching or deep personal relationships. Self-confidence varies, but in a much more subtle way, and over a much longer time. As teachers, we often see this as children who, at the beginning of their basic education, radiate certainty and curiosity, over the years start to shine a little less brightly as the harsh reality of school exams, less than favourable test results, and the onslaught of homework deadlines begin to pile up. Their confidence levels, the external drivers, may still speak of a belief in the ability to achieve, however, the internal awareness and self-speak is completely the opposite. Compare the seven-year-old's belief of invincibility with the 13-year-old's confessions of "I'm not very good at maths"...

In the same way, your confidence levels may profess that you are a capable and energetic leader, yet your self-confidence echoes a nagging voice of doubt. This again is quite normal, and a less than towering inner assessment and belief is no reason for

APPLIED LEADERSHIP IN EDUCATION

you to abandon your aspiration to become a masterful leader. However, the more significant the disparity between your external confidence and your self-confidence, the more energy is wasted on maintaining your confidence levels. And before you realise it, you (and those you are leading) begin to notice that your candle is burning a little less bright as time goes along.

Symptoms of Low Self-confidence

You may find as you become more aware of your emotions you also become more aware of your inner voice. And it would not be strange to suddenly realise that your inner voice is not as confident and self-assured of your ability to lead and grow. This is not a sudden oscillation in your self-confidence, but rather a result of you becoming more aware of your inner world.

You may find that you suddenly realise that the sense of accomplishment with every success no longer reaches such a high point as before. You may notice that the joy of promotion, possession and position are lower and not as long lasting as before. You may become aware that the "lows" of confidence go more in-depth and leave you more disappointed after inevitable failures, and that failure has become personal rather than general and something to learn from. These are all symptoms of low self-confidence.

Building Self-confidence

You may feel that there is nothing wrong with your self-confidence. And that might very well be so. But remember getting better never stops and the first step to growing your inner voice is by clarifying your purpose and meaningfulness. Why are you a school leader? Why have you set on this wavering and often lonely path? What purpose does being the leader in your school have? Moreover, what personal and emotional meaning do you attach to your school, the well-being of students and staff? These are not easy questions to answer, and even the most seasoned of leaders find it difficult to be clear and concise about their purpose and meaningfulness.

The second step is to take a step back and look at the five aspects of your leadership that differentiate you from others. By being aware of what sets you aside, by knowing what those aspects of your professional and personal development that raises you out among the trees are, will help you build a solid foundation on which you can build your self-confidence. To have a clear view of what sets you apart I want you to draw five columns with the following five headings: experience, expertise, knowledge, ability and qualifications. Fill out each of these columns, not with those aspects that you are better than others, but all of those aspects you have. Remember this is not a comparative exercise. Now take an objective look at these differentiating factors. The combination of which is unlike any other school leader on this planet. This is what makes you unique and ready to lead. I am not saying that there is no room for improvement. To the contrary, this activity can also be beneficial to help you determine which aspects of your career you should be working on next.

The last, and probably the most difficult step to developing your self-confidence I found in a little airport bookstore. And with all the simplicity and conciseness one might expect from a book intended to encourage reflection while navigating immigration. Notwithstanding its brevity, I do believe the following ten steps are worth consigning to daily practice alongside your other leadership habits:

- focus on positive self-talk;
- do not compare yourself to others;
- be active, get extra exercise;
- perfection is overrated;
- mistakes are useful to learn from;
- focus on the things you can change and control;
- do things you enjoy, in the way you enjoy;
- celebrate small victories;
- be kind, considerate and helpful (you'll be surprised with the impact of kindness on self-confidence);
- surround yourself with positive people.

Flexibility

As a school leader, you have to deal with an uneasy marriage of adaptability and rigid accountability. Because you are working with the hearts and minds of teachers and young people, you have to consider the individual traits, abilities and developmental progress of everybody, and yet you have a moral imperative to produce academic and progress results that enables every child to be ready for the world of further education and training, the world of work, and to be ready to be a moral and ethical citizen in democratic societies. If you put it like that, it is little wonder that leadership in education is such a difficult job.

School leaders have a particularly difficult time in finding the right balance between flexibility and having a hard hand on the teaching, learning and assessment behaviour of teachers and support staff. On the one hand, if you are seen as flexible, stakeholders very quickly conjure up the image of a leader that is popularity-focussed or consensus-driven. In education, such an approach will sooner than later end up in ineffective teaching and learning. The contrary is also true. A school leader that rules through rigidly holding to the letter of the law, often self-inflicted laws it must be said, will very soon find one-half of the teachers in passive-aggressive rebellion and the other half suffering from burnout.

Flexibility is not renouncing the non-negotiable aspects of being part of a school. It is unthinkable to be flexible with the procedures regarding safeguarding, high expectations of staff and students, integrity and honesty of all stakeholders, continuously driving towards a fully inclusive and richly diversified school, the mastery of teaching, learning and assessment practices and the care and compassion that fosters healthy interpersonal relationships. However, it is your duty as school leader to consider and be amenable towards initiatives that will reduce paperwork, or how to incorporate new technology into the curriculum. I suggest four areas that may help you establish a clear line between the aspects you are open to negotiation and the non-negotiables that are not even open to discussion. You should be open to new ideas, methods and technology. Certain situation and procedures, no matter how established in the school culture can always be reviewed and open to initiates. Letting go of a process or program that you believe in and have fostered for some time isn't always easy, yet leading through listening is often the best way forward to sustain enthusiasm and growth/ progress-based momentum. When it comes to unexpected demands, and the possible solutions to not infringe on the listed non-negotiables I have mentioned above, you should always be open to out-of-the-box solutions and finally, change strategies are not cast in stone. If it becomes clear that a strategy is a burden, you should adapt the method without losing sight of the vision.

Empathy

There is not much to say about your ability to feel empathy as a key personal trait as a school leader. For me, the purpose and meaning that is encapsulated in the job description of a school leader stem from a sincere and earnest empathy you have for the young people under your charge. Your ability to place yourself in their shoes, walk the mile in their context and, let's face it, the stormy waves of hormone changes and inevitable disappointment of growing up, is what will make you a masterful school leader. If you do not have the capacity for such an all-encompassing empathy, I suggest you consider investment banking or carpentry as alternative professions.

As with most traits in this chapter, empathy is not the most straightforward of constructs. Your understanding of empathy may include cognitive empathy, the ability to imagine yourself in the same situation as another person and to see a situation from their point of view. Emotional empathy implies that you can feel the emotions of the other person. Being concerned, is one step removed from the literal experiencing another's emotions, yet through being concerned, you can identify with the emotional state somebody else is experiencing. You may be able to recognise similar experiences and remember what you experienced, and those memories arouse in you a sense of empathy. Finally, you may directly experience the same situation and through your own immediate experiences identify with another person's experiences and emotional states. To be a good and growing

17

school leader, you don't have to burst out in tears if a teacher confides his stress at work and home due to an illness in the family, however, you should have the cognitive and emotional capacity to imagine yourself in a similar situation, even if you have never experienced one yourself.

Without such a capacity of empathy, you are bound to become an ineffective leader, if only because of the reputation of cold-heartedness that will follow in your wake. That being said, not all of us have the same blend of nature and nurture that makes having empathy easy. I suggest that you add the following habits to the list we discussed earlier in this chapter. To cultivate empathy, you should develop curiosity about strangers, especially those that are not from the same socio-economic or cultural groups you find yourself in. Always challenge prejudice, your own as well as the prejudice you see in the people around you. Always look for commonalities with others, again especially with those that you don't find in your immediate proximity. Listen. Listen hard. Listen deep and listen to understand, not to reply. Be an active agent for social change and develop an ambitious imagination through which you see a world that, in any other circumstance would be difficult to achieve. All of this is only possible if you can put aside your viewpoint, try to see all the other perspectives that may apply to a situation, challenge your assumptions and validate the other person's perspective. This is not always easy to do, but remember I am not asking you to disavow your beliefs, change your point of view or render your perspective invalid. To the contrary, holding fast to your convictions is one of the core aspects that I started with at the onset of this chapter. Developing empathy rarely results in you changing your beliefs. However, it often contributes to a richer and more nuanced understanding of the world we live in and the school that you are leading. And that can only be a good thing.

Exit Reflection

Leadership is a deeply personal and exposing voyage to embark on. When you set out to become a leader of any kind, but especially a leader in education, you can expect a lonely and demanding journey that will bare your strengths and weaknesses in ways and times that you will find deeply private. And it will expose these aspects of who you are on ways that most will consider to be unfair and even down right prejudicial. You will often stand alone as the mainstay of a ship that, notwithstanding the tempests of political onslaught, the torrents of ideological change and the winds of social change, have to remain on course to positively impact the lives of other people's children. A Herculean task if ever that was one.

If you have read this far, I am confident that you have chosen leadership as your next step in an honourable career. The first of many more steps of self-development, alongside which you have started on a journey of self-discovery and personal growth.

Dr Jacques Mostert

II

PURPOSE AND LEADERSHIP

If you ask any teacher what they do, the answer is clear. Their response may range from an excited explanation of how they guide children to become curious and enquiring members of society, all the way to a lecture on the amount of assessment and grading they do until small hours of every night. Teachers also don't find any difficulty in flooding any conversation with tales of their teaching, and the inexplicability of children's behaviour in class, how ridiculous some parents are and how much they are in need of a holiday. However, when we ask teachers why they do what they do, the answers become a bit more generic. Because I love working with children is the staple answer, and that may be interjected with a non-descript reference with regular holidays.

Some teachers may be very clear that they put up with the mountains of grading and the odd disruptive student because they "want to make a difference", but not often do even these self-aware teacher expand on why they want to make a

21

difference.

This lack of clear understanding and plain statement of why teachers do their job is not limited to the education industry only. It is concerning that those who have our children's future, as the very future of society, in their hands do not have a clear understanding of why they are doing what they are doing. What is even more concerning is that if you ask a range of school leaders, you will probably find similar answers as that of the teachers they are supposed to lead.

If I were to ask you why you are a school leader, or why you want to become a school leader, your answer may include wanting to make your school better or give learners the opportunity to thrive. However, the question remains un-answered. Why would you want to make lives of children, who you don't know that much, better? Why would you want them to thrive? The reason I am starting this book with asking you what your purpose of being or becoming a school leader is, includes the fact that if you don't have clarity of your purpose, It will be somewhat difficult to recognise and clearly communicate the overarching purpose of your school.

Purpose of Leadership in Education

There isn't always a perfect answer for the purpose you have in becoming a leader in education. An appropriate response would probably include the moral imperative you have to create a climate and culture of care, community and well-being in your school. You may include the effect of our innate drive for self-determination, or you may expand on the fact that we are programmed to protect the species, and creating effective schools where our young can thrive, is part of providing such protection. I suspect that such diatribes would be taking things too far.

As you can see, finding purpose in your role as teacher and as a school leader is not as easy as one might think once confronted with the question. I suspect the purpose of being a teacher can be found somewhere on the spectrum between "because I like children" and "for the survival of the species".

Luckily, the question of the purpose of your school is more or less answered through its very definition. A place where young people can learn to become contributing members of democratic societies. If this is the answer to what the purpose of your school is, then why even have the discussion? The fact is that schools, like individuals, communities and society as a whole, are not homogenous. However, there is a difference between the vision, mission and purpose of the school. In my mind, the purpose comes first. Purpose, in short, is why your school is in the business of teaching and learning. The vision is how you see this purpose being actualised and the mission is what you are doing to actualise the vision. Goals are more specific and short-term and they are supported by target areas and behaviours. Your purpose remains stable, immovable, whereas the vision, mission strategies and goals are more responsive to changing situations and environments to actualise the purpose of the school.

There are several reasons why purpose forms one of the first chapter of this book and the place where you should start your journey into leadership. Firstly, how well you, as the school leader, give your teachers a sense of purpose at work, profoundly influences how well they will perform their duties. Teachers that are deeply engaged in the teaching, learning and assessment of their students are also those who have a sincere sense of purpose. Those teachers are more productive, self-driven and take account-ability for their performance, whereas it doesn't take much for teachers who are ambiguous about their purpose to feel exhausted and burnt out. As a matter of fact, those teachers, and school leaders for that matter, who have the strongest sense of purpose have more positive emotions, are more enthusiastic, have an optimistic outlook and contentment. Those who do not, are three times more likely to feel worried, stressed, gloomy, depressed and abjectly miserable. It doesn't take much convincing to admit that being the leader of the first group of teachers will be a much more natural and pleasurable job, than the latter.

There is no one-size-fits-all solution to what role a school plays in its host community, and there is no mould according to which your school could be cast to ensure success. Your purpose as the leader in your school is to establish, clarify and com-municate the purpose of the school, and through your leadership behaviours, you should ensure that the purpose of the school is actualised.

The remainder of this book is dedicated to providing you with the understanding of how to facilitate your teachers, staff and students to realise the specific purpose of your school. All the chapters are set out to provide you with the skills, attitudes and behaviours that make it possible to achieve this one aspect of the phenomenon of school.

Authentic Purpose

One important problem you may face is understanding and communicating the purpose of the school is found in your own self-serving bias. We all come with our unique package of assumptions, beliefs and biases. And when you enter your role as the leader in your school, these assumptions, beliefs and biases are placed directly in the spotlight, and as much as these aspects of who you are, are magnified, so they become part and parcel of what you presume to be the purpose of the school. Authentic purpose is the attempt to navigate your understanding of the school's purpose past these assumptions, beliefs and biases and find the authentic, real-world purpose of the school.

To establish your school's purpose you should determine what it is that your school community needs, what they aspire to, where they see themselves in future. Tap into their self-determination and dreams. Talk with them, and listen to learn from them, rather than inform them of what they should espouse. The most successful schools and by association the most successful leaders are those that place their customers first: the students, parents and broader school community. The school's purpose becomes indistinguishable from that of its community. Relevance is imperative.

Behaviours of Purposeful Leaders

The most important behaviour of a leader that imbues purpose is making her/his teachers and support staff feel important and appreciated. If you spend time and effort to recognise your teachers for their effort and the significant role they play in actualising the purpose of the school, they will not only perform better but quite often be inspired to make their students feel appreciated and important. In short, happy teachers make for happy students.

Spreading appreciation isn't the only attribute that is significant to the actualisation of the school's purpose. You must also be good at communicating the vision and purpose of the school, and this can only be done if you have clarity of what that purpose is. You must have a clear understanding of how your values contribute to the behaviours of your teachers, and that genuinely valuing their contributions and effort is the locomotive that drives the actualising process of the school. To be genuinely appreciative of teachers' effort, you must look and listen, not look to be able to direct or correct behaviour but rather to recognise and appreciate how their behaviours contribute to the school's purpose. Your teachers' perspectives are valuable, and because they are on the frontline of fulfilling the purpose of your school, their voice is indisputably as crucial as that of the students and their parents.

You must encourage your teachers and staff to become masterful at what they do for them to be true to why they do it. You must show through your actions and language that you care about the school's vision, values and purpose. You must help teachers and support staff see where the school is headed, what you want them to achieve collectively. Your behaviours must be directed to making teachers, and staff feel like their contribution to the purpose of the school is important and that without their effort, the purpose cannot be actualised.

You must listen to learn and not the other way around. Through demonstrating that you understand the teachers' needs and valuing their input and perspectives, you confirm the significance of their role in making the school and its students thrive. And naturally, none of these behaviours is important if you negate your commitments and don't deliver on your promises.

Values are Valuable

Through the behaviours we discussed above, you will create a climate and culture of purpose in your school. The values that you collectively hold becomes the signature of your school's reputation. You must ensure that the values, beliefs in action, that you choose for your school help to deliver a positive contribution to the relationships, reputation and results of the school. We all know of schools that are reputed for being unrelenting in academic rigour, or exclusive to a fault, or even for being the breeding ground of distrust and despair.

Values should help your school to achieve its vision, goals and its purpose. The values you espouse to and your purpose are inexorably linked, and if there is dissonance between your beliefs in action and the purpose and vision of your school, you will pretty soon start to experience the wheels coming off the proverbial wagon. As the leader, it is your duty to ensure that your teachers, staff and students live the values of the school through their attitudes and actions. However, it isn't easy to decide on a set of core values that will empower teachers and staff to help create a positive, purpose-driven climate and culture.

There are six places where you can seek to find the values that will help you develop the school's climate and culture. The first is operational values of the school. These are linked to the day-to-day activities and behaviours of all stakeholders. Honesty, academic integrity, care, respect and curiosity are but a few values that cannot be left off your list. The second are values of diversity, that celebrates the individuality of each as well as the uniqueness of your school. These values of diversity are closely related to the purpose of your school: as mentioned above, no school is ever alike. You should ask yourself, what is it that your school does differently? How do you add value to the education and well-being of your students and staff? These values are fundamental and should be kept alive to keep the path towards actualising your propose. Thirdly, you should consider values that will make your school a caring and inclusive environment to be part of. What makes it a pleasant place to work at and what makes it a school your students are proud of? In the fourth place, you should be very clear about your performance values. How are you creating students and staff that aspire to accountability, agility, commitment and critical thinking? In the fifth place, you must include your personal values into you set or core values. Your beliefs in action will manifest whether you want them to or not, and if they are at odds with the values embraced by the school, then you are in for a difficult time. Finally, you must always keep both eyes on the here and now as well as on the future. If you think about it, you will realise that the present moment in any school is the future. What you are doing now in your school will play no small part in the future development and culture of the broader school community. If your active beliefs are that of inclusion, curiosity and care, before long you will start recognising these values manifesting in your school community.

Exit Reflection

As the leader, you are the guardian of the authentic purpose of your school, and you must be unrelenting about ensuring that the school's purpose is actualised. Your job, in a nutshell, is to make the authentic purpose of the school actual and tangible.

A strong set of values, (that are aligned with the purpose, vision and goals of the school) alongside an anchored purpose energises teachers and support staff, and a climate and culture that make teachers and support staff happy will lead your students and parents to be happy.

The key steps you need to take are:

- develop a clear understanding of the authentic purpose of the school;
- define the values that will navigate your actions as well as the behaviours of your teachers, staff and students;
- improve your own ability to engage with your customers (parents and students) teachers and support staff;
- create alignment between the purpose, vision, mission, values and strategic goals of your school;
- measure progress towards actualising purpose and be relentless in your behaviours to actualise the purpose;
- communicate, communicate, communicate.

Dr Jacques Mostert

III

TEACHING AND LEADING

There seems to be a growing international crisis in education: teachers are leaving the profession, schools are failing their students and increasing numbers of young people remain unemployed for longer after leaving school. Governments are increasingly becoming anxious about holding teachers accountable while finding ways to increase class sizes without empowering teachers more, and increasing expectations, without paying teachers more. The speed at which new silver-bullet-solutions and inspection regimes are announced, and then changed again, without consideration of the impact such changes may have on students and teachers is ubiquitous. And in the wake of it all, are the young people that are more confused about what they should be able to do and know, and when they should be able to demonstrate their ability to do it. You will be forgiven for thinking that education has become nothing more than a fast-paced exercise in ambiguity and that it seems that everybody has a different opinion of how to steer it.

Notwithstanding the vast list of complaints about the lack of professional behaviour of teachers, unengaged and often down-right dismal student behaviour, parental indifference, rampant technological advances and the dialectic dualism of those in government, it's not surprising that there are calls for scrapping the whole system and starting all over. However, if you take a step back, muffle the cacophony of concerns and look around you, you will see islands of educational success stories that hardly ever make the newspaper front pages. These schools are succeeding not because they are being sheltered from adversity, socio-economic stressors and naughty children, they are not successful because they get to choose only the richest, best and brightest students, they are successful not because they get to spend vast amounts of money on the best technology. They are successful because of their leaders have chosen to look past all these impediments and succeed in any case.

Leadership is all about providing clarity of vision and direction, analysing the current context and devising strategies for development, however, no matter how great your strategies are, an excellent strategy without excellent delivery is a waste of time. There is no doubt that the stronger and dynamic the team of people that are involved in the process of developing your school's vision, including your students, their parents, other school leaders, teachers and support staff, the greater the sense of ownership in that vision will be. However, it comes down to you, the leader in your school, notwithstanding the level at which you take leadership or hold accountability for, that is the driving force of making the vision a reality.

Successful schools have clearly defined goals that are not only challenging to achieve, but are also aspiring and that seek to show not only the students, but the whole school community what levels they can achieve. The worst thing you as a leader can do is set a generic vision, and easily obtainable goals that the teachers students and parents don't understand or identify with.

It is important that everyone that is involved with the school understands what their personal role in achieving the goals are, and how each person's part is essential to achieve the goals the school wants to achieve for its students. And that is where the role and purpose of leadership in education comes in. It is your job to make sure every person that is involved in the education process knows what to do, when to do it, where and how it should be done in order to ensure that every child has the very best opportunity to develop and thrive. Without you leading from the front, it is virtually impossible for a school to rise up to levels of excellence and mastery.

The Anatomy of School

The construct of school, schooling, and the place you call your school, is a uniquely human creation. Nowhere else in nature do we find an organism that willingly, even deliberately, places the care of their young in the hands of strangers with the trust that those strangers will take care of these offspring as if they are their own. Zoologists and ecologists may raise attention to a few species that collectively raise their young. They may even ask what about marine animals that don't raise their young, and the answer lies in the questions, they don't raise their offspring: their endurance as a species depends on numbers and the roll of the survival *of the fittest* dice. Lions, elephants and dolphins make use of their pride, herd or shoal to protect their progeny, but that happens in established groups, where strangers are seldom allowed to join the group. It is indeed, inimitably human to place our trust and expectation of doing a good job of educating our children in the hands of people that, in many cases, do not even reside within our communities.

As humans, we have attached a moral imperative to the school, an existential prerogative that those in charge of the care and education of our children are of a higher moral standing, of greater ethical awareness, of superior psychological and emotional immovability, of infinite patience, of nobler disposition, of limitless capacity for fairness and social justice, the unwavering acuity to recognising the matchlessness of each child and, of whom it can be said that at the core of their character, they hold an optimism that looks beyond the current zeitgeist (spirit of the times) and sees the hope that is inextinguishable in a new generation. In simple terms, we place the future of our communities and the continued existence of our species in the hands of humans, that for all intents and purposes, cannot actually exist. And herein lies the very essence of your calling (yes, I used the word calling) to become a school leader.

Leading and Teaching: Responsibility and Accountability

Leadership can be described in terms of two functions: providing direction and exercising influence. Yet when we start to look at all the constituent parts of leadership in education we realize that the sum of the parts falls far short from the responsibility encapsulated in the whole. This is not a modern phenomenon. Leadership in education is held to equal or higher standards than captains of industry. Where industry has profit as one over-arching aim, leaders in education are responsible and accountable for a range of interlinking performance, moral, social and individual obligations. In 1913 Bobbitt wrote "with scales of measurement and standards of performance . . . , it is no longer possible for a principal to hide behind the plea that he (sic) has an inferior social class in his school, and, therefore, high performance should not be expected of him or of his teachers."

Some leadership roles are clearly defined, and others may emerge over time as teachers interact with their peers, showing passion and dedication that is not tied to a job description. However, you may think about your role as energising and calling those around you to action. The role of a leader in school cannot be divorced from the ultimate outcomes of its students: excellent leadership leads to excellent progress and outcomes.

The demands on educational leaders are constantly evolving. To prepare yourself to face such demands and develop the change in education that is needed to provide the very best TLA environment for all your staff and students, you need to understand what the role of educational leadership involves.

Leadership is seen as not about *doing to* others, but rather about what develops from the way leaders *do with* others. In other words, how you work with and relate to others, as colleagues will determine the success you have as a leader. Leadership in education is an ongoing process and must be seen within a context of the community the school serves. Understanding and improving human behaviour is key to leadership, however, it doesn't merely have influence over followers, it also has responsibility for their well-being, and it is this responsibility that places leadership in education on a higher moral imperative.

Difference Between Leadership and Management

To be a leader, you must have followers. You can be as dynamic, dedicated and even charismatic as the best of leaders, yet without somebody to lead, you are by definition, not a leader. The importance of followers and the role your followers will play in your leadership skills, attitudes and capacity cannot be understated. It is true, in many cases, especially schools, many followers have no choice but to follow. However, does this mean that they are following you as a leader or are they merely going through the motions, tolerating the inconvenience of *following* a leader and at times coping despite the incompetence of the leader? School leadership can very easily become like two ships in the night, narrowly passing one another without noticing much more than a slight swell in the wake of the other. We traditionally consider school leadership in terms of managers that place emphasis on rule conformance and the relationships between the manager and teacher is founded on that of institutionalised authority.

Managers Insist On Hierarchy, Leaders Are In Service Of Their Followers

Management is organisation centred with duties and activities clearly set out and monitored according to specific measures. Schools have evolved into organisations with complex hierarchical structures that are based on superior and subordinate roles of individuals. These roles depend on how complex or overarching the responsibility of the post holder is, and each of these hierarchical posts have legal, formal authority as well as income differences attached to the role. In this bureaucratic system, interpersonal relationships are based on formal and fixed hierarchies with specific levels of power, perceived privilege and decision-making authority drives the interactions between people. In other words, *if you want to get your pay, you will do what I say.*

Managers Use Authority, Leaders Build Relationships

Leadership, despite having monitoring of rule conformity built into the role, places emphasis on the interpersonal relationships that are fostered between the leader and the follower. Leadership looks at the school not in terms of a bureaucratic behemoth, but through the eyes of humans with individual needs, aspirations and driving forces. The difference between a leader and a manager is that a leader uses the vision of mutually beneficial outcomes as the magnet that pulls the follower closer, whereas the manager uses the rule book to push people to outcomes they do not necessarily believe in. The authority that is ascribed to a leader is based on capability, moral integrity and democratic values. In other words, *a leader doesn't need the rule book to point the way.* Leadership aims to fill teaching as a profession with a sense of meaning, worth and validity that are based on the values to which a community, and society at large aspires. The entire community, not only the school, benefits from successful leadership in education, and a key factor of leadership is that a central part of being a leader is to empower followers to become leaders.

Managers Follow Inflexible Rules, Leaders Have Moral Authority

Leaders are driven by the moral authority at the heart of a cause; the context of the specific situation; the need for transformation of emerging societies and the ongoing improvement of communal human existence. Based on this humanistic approach to leadership, the psychology of human motivation plays and important role in becoming a successful leader, and therefore the fundamentals of psychology are woven into the theory and application of leadership. Without a knowledge of human emotions and motivation, you will in the first place not be able to understand yourself and what drives you, nor would you be able to understand the people follow your direction.

Managers Have Limited Remit, Leader Share Collective Social Responsibility

Leadership in education involves working with teachers, students and other education professionals in order to implement and sustain the constant improvement of TLA in order for every child to be able to achieve their highest and most authentic selves. The leadership roles in education are not limited to the school, local authority or department of education. With the emergence of online education, education leadership has started to include entrepreneurs, motivational speakers such as Sir Ken Robertson and Simon Sinek as well as corporations that expand their social responsibility into the realm of education leadership.

However, there is also a dark side of leadership to be aware of. The same personality traits that contribute to some leaders to be seen as attractive and worthy to follow, such as charisma, inspiration, vision, courage, and resilience, can also become a destructive force to those around them. If there is a lack of empathy and concern for the people that the leader works with; or, a lack of understanding of the impact the leader has on the people surrounding her; or, an unwillingness to take responsibility, leadership can become the poison that slowly breaks down the school community and even society at large.

Responsibilities of Leaders in Education

The most important responsibility of education leadership is to improve the lives of the young people in your charge. This is not only implied by the ethos of *in loco parentis* insofar as *leadership is second only to classroom instruction as an influence on student learning*.

Responsibility for Teaching and Learning

There is a clear link between the effective leadership practices and provision of high-quality teaching, learning and assessment (TLA), whether teacher-directed or teacher-guided. To be able to influence the outcomes of classroom pedagogy, leaders are expected to understand the principles of quality TLA and to have appropriate knowledge of the curriculum to guarantee that appropriate content is being delivered to all students. This presumes leaders are capable of providing constructive feedback to improve TLA. Therefore, to enable progress and positive change, the role of educational leaders may include to:

- analyse student data and observe classes to pinpoint potential problems and areas for improvement;
- build effective supportive professional relationships;
- develop and improve organisational structure;

- manage budgets and implement financial accountability;
- develop, implement and continuously evaluate school policy and procedures;
- hire, evaluate and manage human capital;
- research new and effective TLA strategies;
- uphold curriculum standards;
- work to reform education on the local, state or national level.

School leadership spearheads efforts to shape school conditions through setting clear goals, culture and structures. Classroom conditions, are influenced through the direction and motivation of school leadership and aspects of TLA that are influenced by the competency of a school's executive leadership team include:

- the content of the curriculum;
- setting academic objectives to establish high expectations;
- using specific strategies for managing TLA opportunities inside as well as outside of the classroom;
- researching and implementing appropriate instruction methods conducive to the characteristics of the students;
- manage resources to sustain appropriate numbers of students in classrooms;
- model and encourage inclusive policy and practices by teachers.

Responsibility for Student Progress, Safety and Holistic Development of Each Individual

The primary client of a school is the student, and the primary function of a school is to be a safe place where each student can develop their capacity to grow, to thrive and set out on a journey of authentic self-determination. At the heart of leadership lies accountability for safety and well-being of students and staff, the continuous development of high academic standards, and continuous improvement of an inclusive TLA environment. As the leader of this weighty endeavour, your first and utmost responsibility lies in safeguarding each and every student. It is your moral imperative to ensure that every child is safe to learn, safe to make mistakes, safe to explore their inner being, safe to become a fully functioning human being. If this seems like an unachievable task, then education leadership is not for you.

Responsibility to Contribute to Developing the School Community

Accountability is usually driven through data-analyses, reporting progress to stakeholders and successful outcomes of inspections. However, education leadership also carries with it moral accountability that is not so easily captured through data analyses or inspection reports. Your role as leader also includes how the school contributes to the fabric of society, through producing young people that become responsible, contributing members of society. School improvement depends on a collaborative approach to leadership, which includes com-municating findings, failures, and concerns.

Responsibility for Relationship-building

Relationship building is imperative to effective school leadership. A true leader will create a TLA environment in which opportunities for positive change are present and supported throughout the school. In clearer terms, *if you take care and develop your teachers, your teachers will take care of and develop their students.* Trust is one of the most significant parts of building interpersonal relationships and as predictor of the success of the school. Trust in the leadership of the school, is a better indicator of how effective a school is than teacher participation in decision making. Therefore, it is vitally important that the teachers, students, parents and community trust the decision-making capability of the leadership in the school in order to cultivate a sense of overall approval with the school. In addition, developing positive relationships among staff (teachers, administrative and support staff) encourages supportive school-wide professional networks that enables them to take on various supplementary roles with one another. Such interactions include being a mentor or mentee, a skills coach, modelling specialist teaching, and advising on curriculum content, TLA strategies as well as dealing with individual students.

Responsibility for Establishing and Modelling Core Values

Professional networks make up more than just support. It also includes sharing the core values of the school, having a common focus on high expectations, taking collective re-sponsibility for student learning and well-being, actively and purposefully reflecting on improvement, and the persistent sharing of effective TLA practices—all of which may be thought of as forms of leadership.

Ethics and Values in Education Leadership

A leader in education is a person that endlessly works towards promoting the success of all students by acting with integrity, fairness and in an ethical way. As a leader in education you are driven by a moral purpose, and you are guided by the ethics and values of society at large. In theory, this sounds correct, and as leader you most certainly aspire to be a moral and ethical leader, but what does building your leadership behaviours on ethics on morals actually look like. Who do you look up to? How do you implement being a moral and ethical leader?

Firstly, you must find clarification on what is meant by ethics, values and morals in education. It is only by forming solid knowledge and understanding of what these aspects of leadership mean that you can know how to implement them in your leadership behaviour. Ethics are the principles or internal rules according to which you behave when you are engaged with an activity. According to these internal rules you will have a belief of what is the *right* (upstanding and morally correct, good) way of doing something and what is the wrong (immoral or harmful) way of doing something.

The word ethics comes from Greek and originally it meant *habits* or *the way you always do things.* In short, the habit you have of behaving in either an upstanding or a harmful way. Deciding on your own ethics, is one of the most important first steps on your journey into leadership.

There is a much more complex conversation to be held about what ethics and morals mean in different societies and even communities within society (what is morally correct in one society could be exactly what is sinful and immoral in another). An example of this could be the education of girls. In the majority of the developed world, it is a moral imperative to provide equal quality education for boys and girls. However, in some societies, the concept of educating a girl is considered to be wrong, or even immoral. Depending on where you find yourself at this very point in time, you will have a view on this example. Based on your religion, race and culture, you may understand why some societies insist on girls being educated in the skills of home making and boys educated at school.

Ethics in Education

For you to be able to determine which ethical framework and which specific values you embrace, you must have a knowledge and understanding of a) the various ethical frameworks and perspectives, and b) the professional codes of conduct and underlying principles of education. When you have developed an understanding of these two prerequisites, you must explore your own beliefs and values and then establish your own ethical code that will guide your leadership behaviours.

Despite sounding very philosophical and even a bit intangible, having a stated and even publically known ethical code, written down and available for yourself and other to see is the very first step towards becoming a successful leader. There is a very simple reason for actually writing down your personal code of ethics: *when the hurley burley's done and the battle is lost and won*, it is easy to look past what you believe in and merely react to situations. If you have a clearly stated and visible code of ethics, it is easy to face the complex mix of making decisions, providing direction and being fair in your judgement, when you and others can see what you believe in. Therefore, the first step of applying leadership to your role is to clarify your values and write down your code of ethics.

The main objective of having a code of ethics is to determine what is right and what is wrong. This is built on virtues such as honesty, justice, fairness, courage, empathy, integrity and kindness. Ethics are seen in terms of social justice, and considers the inequalities that exist based on gender, race, social and economic class, the orientation towards who you love and the identity you feel most closely to. There are four ethical frameworks that you should understand in order to develop your won ethical code: ethics of justice, ethics of critique, ethics of care and concern as well as the ethics that are specific to education as a profession.

Ethic of Justice

The ethics of justice is based on democratic principles and relates to education, freedom and the right of self-determination. Thus, the ethics of justice will consider a commitment to the development of humans in order to increase equality of opportunity, equality under the law and the right to choose. Under the ethics of justice procedures and policies are developed to guide decisions in such a way that equality and the rights of individuals are reinforced. Words and ideas such as justice, fairness, laws and rights are used as the foundation of ethics of justice. Policies and procedures are designed to be objective, impartial and in a step-by-step way in order to empower all humans to achieve their personal freedom and self-actualization.

In real terms this means that your school will be based on democratic principles and the policies that guide the actions of leadership, teachers, students, parents and support staff will encourage full participation in decision-making, and im- plementing the vision and inclusive education opportunities. Fairness and kindness will guide the actions and behaviour of all people in the school and there will be explicit policies that are seen to be implemented to counteract any discrimination or bullying. Equal education opportunities will form the foundation of high academic and behaviour expectations from everybody in the school (including the leadership) to advance social justice and social mobility. Students and staff will know their rights and they will have the opportunity to apply those rights without the fear of recrimination or punishment. Students and staff will have clear responsibilities to contribute to the democratic ethos of the school and they will be held accountable alongside the leadership of the school to advance the ethics of justice.

Ethic of Critique

The ethics of critique accept democracy and liberal values but it places emphasis on critique of the laws, rules processes and standards that are established. There is tension between what is considered to be just and establishing if the laws and rules are actually just. Rather than accepting the established ethics of those in power, leaders that follow the ethics of critique actively engage in questions about fairness and justice of the policies and rules in the school. They ask hard questions about how students and staff are treated and engage in discussions about how to deal with the paradoxes in the implementation of those rules. They are acutely aware of how our own morals and values can become corrupted over time for the sake of practicality or convenience, thus forcing us to rethink important concepts such as democracy, social justice, privilege, and power.

At school the ethics of critique will question the validity of excluding a student from lessons because he has broken the uniform rule. How ethical is it to bar a student from assessments because of jewellery rules of sending them home for being late to class? Despite the fact that the ethics of justice may have followed a democratic process to determine the school rules, the ethics of critique actively question the justness of those rules.

Ethic of Care, Concern, and Connectedness

Leaders that place the ethics of care, concern and connectedness follow a humanistic foundation in their approach to ethics. In the same way as the ethics of critique, they question the validity of established laws and the dominant ethics of society. However, the ethics of care, concern and connectedness looks towards empathy and humanness to challenge the established patriarchy. They see the responsibility all humans have for the well-being of the other as a key responsibility and they focus on inter personal relationships to lead discussions of continuity, respect, trust and empowerment.

At school the ethics of care, concern and connectedness is mostly found with those who work directly with the well-being and pastoral care of students. This includes holding leaders, teachers, students and support staff accountable for the way they interact with those who are part of a minority group, those who face adversity or are at risk of adversity and those with special education needs and difficulties. The leader that follows the ethics of care, concern and connectedness will lead discussions on inclusive education practices, staff and student well-being and forming a deep empathy for the individual circumstances and context of each individual in the school. In practice, these leaders insist on an individual approach to every situation.

Ethic of the Profession

It is the responsibility of leaders in education to provide the opportunity and freedom for each individual in the school to form their own ethical code of conduct based on their experiences, expectations critical events and personal context. In the same way as leaders aim to empower others to develop a code of ethics, the leadership team should establish and demonstrate their own personal code of ethics. In practice, a leader may feel the pressure of having the leadership team *sing of the same hymn sheet* or to follow a uniform code of ethics. However, this is contradictory to the very nature of a code of ethics. There is a difference between a code of conduct and the ethics that drive our individual behaviour. There are however codes of ethics that are central to each profession, and in the case of education these may include inclusiveness, social mobility, developing self-determination and the clear aim to place the best interest of the student at the centre of all school activities.

Ethics in the Classroom

Teachers must conduct themselves as responsible professionals at all times with *honesty, integrity, fairness, impartiality* and *kindness*. To engender a school that not only prepares its students to achieve the expected academic standards but also form its young people to become a new generation of contributing members of society, we must infuse the classroom with the ethical values we want them to live by. Tomorrow's entrepreneurs, lawyers, medical professionals, researchers and teachers, service personnel and technicians, communication specialists and, thinkers and artists, musicians and, more important than ever, politicians must have a solid moral compass based on ethical values that make society at large a better place for everybody.

It is true that classrooms, corridors, display areas, the staff room and play areas should become a picture of moral language such as *courage, honesty, kindness, carefulness, patience* and *compassion*. A teacher's first moral responsibility is to the students in his/her care. The behaviours of teacher in their classroom make their ethics and values clear.

You may have plastered the corridor walls with slogans of morality and hung the schools code of ethics from the rafters, however, it is the day-to-day modelling of these ethics and values that will remain engrained in students' memories. Let me give you an example. I find it sadly ironic to see a young person outside a classroom, having been sent out because he took a bite from his sandwich, sitting under a poster that propagates kindness and compassion. In explanation of his situation, the young man explains that he did not have time to eat breakfast because of his mother's illness, and that he was hungry. He didn't think the teacher would see him eat in class. Such anecdotal evidence of, what can only be described as institutional hypocrisy (our values statements announces care; however, the unyielding rules are uncaring) can be found in every school you will set foot in.

Teaching is described as a caring profession through which *justice, trust, integrity* and *truth* are developed. These are all very powerful words, and in theory may form the spine of what we do as teachers, it may be the personal values that uphold you as a leader and the personal traits you want to be the hallmark of your life. However, the minute a teacher enters the trenches of the frontline (especially after lunchbreak) all bets are off and it is more often than not the survival of the fittest that counts, and it is how one behaves when under pressure that will reveal one's true ethics, values and beliefs.

In the playground and after school, you want the community to say that your school is the expression of *respect for others, responsibility, civility, honour* and *balance*. Yet, once the end of the day has come and you make your way down the car park, and out towards the exit, it is the shrapnel of home-time snacks wrappers, abandoned blazers, and inverted book cases with its contents vomited onto the sidewalk that proves that no matter how much these virtues are infused into the curriculum, the evidence of their very existence is scant where children have entered and left. As leader, it is your responsibility to bring the values which want to see actualise in your school off from the posters on the corridor walls and make them manifest in student behaviours.

Gone are the days of *do what I tell you, don't do what I do.* School leaders must be aware that their actions (even more than their beliefs and words) have a fundamentally moral and ethical impact on the people they lead. Teachers will do, what they see you do, and students will act the way they see their teachers act. Therefore, it isn't just you, the leader, that must have a clear understanding of your values and ethical foundations, but also your teachers and support staff. You must encourage them to be acutely aware of their own ethical stance and hold them accountable if their behaviour and stated beliefs do not align. And, where a teacher or support staff member cannot in all good faith hold the ethical values as envisioned by the school, you may have to follow the guidelines and policies to help that teacher find another job.

Ethical Standards for the Teaching Profession

Education as a profession aims to foster the growth and development of dedicated teachers and support staff. The ethical standards or rather, the *ten commandments* of the teaching profession provide you with a baseline for the expectations of all teachers' and support staff's ethical behaviour. Teachers uphold the dignity and honour of the profession through their practice by:

1. upholding professional relationships with their students with integrity, honesty, fairness and dignity;
2. recognizing and respecting the privileged nature of the relationship that teachers maintain with students;
3. establishing impartial and consistent respect for all students as individuals with distinctive and on-going learning needs and capabilities;
4. respecting confidential information about students unless disclosure is required by law or personal safety is at risk;
5. modelling respect for human dignity, spiritual and cultural values, freedom, social justice, democracy and the environment;
6. working cooperatively with peers in the school and others, to create a professional environment that supports the social, physical, emotional, intellectual, spiritual, cultural, moral and ethical development of students;
7. building relationships with parents or guardians in their role as partner in the education of students, on respect, trust, and communication;
8. cooperating with professionals from other agencies in the interest of students as required by law;
9. acting with integrity, honesty, fairness and dignity in all their interactions with their peers;
10. taking care of their own mental, physical and spiritual health.

Again, the proof lies in the pudding, and there will be times that you have to refer to the ethical values that enfold the teaching profession to address some of the TLA behaviours of your teachers and support staff. Most often, the frustration and stress that comes with the over-assessment of outcomes, mountains of administration to prove accountability and creating gallery worthy classroom displays leaves teachers drained to the point where the personal professional relationships with teachers and peers takes a distant third place on the list of priorities.

You need to ask yourself why it is that teachers spend more time preparing the face value aspects of their practice (displays, administration and filing) than building relationships? Why is it that teachers don't know the names of their students' pets or parents (or in some case that they don't have any)? Why is it that teachers revert to aggressive gestures such as shouting and sarcasm in maintaining unnaturally quiet classroom environments (have you ever been in a public space where it is dead still, this type of silence is not natural and save of test conditions, probably not productive either)? All the questions I have asked you are aimed at helping you think about the workload you and the leadership team have piled onto an already emotionally draining profession. In other words, it is your ethical duty to be kind and compassionate (keep additional work load to the minimum and practical, use technology to work for you, not as a barrier); to be fair and maintain dignity (don't use the staffroom meetings to bully and threaten across the board); to encourage balance (use your position to send teachers home, when their family needs them and have at least one no-work Wednesday-afternoon per month); to build professional interpersonal relationships (know the names of your teachers' children or whether they even have children at all).

Your Personal Values as a Leader

Like the ten commandments of ethical teaching practice, you as the leader have ten value types that set the bar for your personal values as a leader.

1. Self-Direction: you must work towards achieving independent thought and action in order to use your own creativity and critical thinking skills to make decisions as well as evaluate the impact of your leadership style, role and expectations from outside the school.
2. Stimulation: to develop confidence and boldness in searching for and encouraging diversification and progressive thinking.
3. Satisfaction: to allow yourself the pleasure of seeing your vision take shape, when students are achieving their highest potential.
4. Stability: espousing to sustain personal and social harmony, consistency in approach and fairness.
5. Constraint: refraining from any impulsive action or deliberate course of action that may cause harm.
6. Respect: recognizing the diversity of beliefs and norms, acknowledge, respect and preserve a common social background.
7. Humanism: promoting and conserving human values, including our human tendency to make mistakes, and our ability to learn from them.
8. Well-being: seeking and encouraging the welfare of the students and staff under your leadership.
9. Universalism: understanding, respecting, tolerating and protecting humans and nature.

10. Health: taking care of your own mental and physical health in such a way that you can return to lead another day.

The Characteristics and Attitudes of Leaders in Education

Effective leaders in education need to develop a high level of emotional intelligence and interpersonal skills. The effectiveness of school leaders depends on their ability to persuade and influence students, staff and the school community, rather than to direct or manage them.

Sir David Woods advises that *"you have to take people with you, you can't be bullish, you have got to build collaboration and get people to work together."* This means that as a leader in education you must have the capacity and interpersonal skills to empower teachers in order for them to learn and grow according to the vision you have set out for the school. It also means that you must have direct and continuous participation alongside teachers to work towards improving TLA. You can only do this if you are acutely aware of the TLA that takes place in the school, the impediments teachers and students face and the capacity building that is needed to improve. Education leadership is not an opportunity to establish your own brand or gain power. It is mostly thankless, time consuming and filled with obstacles that will test many people's resolve. If you, as a leader in the school do not have a) the capacity for collaborative working, b) an unshakeable drive for service towards your students, teachers, support staff and the broader school community, or c) if interpersonal relationships and communication is not your strength, you should ask yourself, why you want to venture into education leadership.

The following set of characteristics shared by successful school leaders are worth thinking about:

1. Effective education leaders (on any level of the leadership ladder) consistently hold high expectations of themselves and others and their ambitions is for the success of their pupils and not for their own sake.
2. Effective leaders constantly demonstrate that economic and social disadvantage need not be a barrier to student academic progress and achievement.
3. They focus uncompromisingly on improving TLA with very effective and targeted professional development of all staff.
4. They have a detailed knowledge of each individual child.
5. They are highly inclusive, and consistently look for opportunities to improve the progress and personal development of every child.
6. They encourage rich learning opportunities, both within and outside of the classroom.
7. They proactively develop positive partnerships particularly with parents, businesses and the community to support pupil learning and progress.
8. They are rigorous in their self-evaluation with clear strategies for progress.
9. They believe that getting better never stops.

The Mindful Leader

Though one of the most applicable aphorisms of school development is that successful leaders focus on the school, and not on themselves, it would be amiss to not spend some time on looking at how you, as the leader, can improve on your own skills in order to become a self-aware and mindful leader. Behind any *expert leader*'s facade is a constantly-questioning, frequently self-doubting, always-improving individual who knows that there is yet a lifetime of room to grow and develop. Only when a leader is mindful and self-aware, can s/he place emphasis on the school, its vision and its needs.

Developing your leadership skills is a continuous process that, no matter for how long you have been in leadership and management, doesn't ever end. Nor does leadership ever get any easier. Let me explain, leadership is often experienced as a very isolating and solitary role, not only because you are often seen as standing out above those you are leading, but also because the ultimate accountability for actualizing the vision and objectives of the school, rests with you. Another reason developing your leadership skills isn't always easy is because, as leader, your followers have a rather unfair expectation that you should be faultless and that any improvement of your own areas of development is seen as a weakness. Admitting that you too have aspects of your leadership skills and behaviour that can and should be developed isn't always easy and requires a great deal of humility and trust on both your part and those that follow you.

Developing Self-awareness

Being self-aware is the ability to have a clear perception of your own personality, including your strengths, weaknesses, thoughts, behaviour, beliefs, knowing what motivates you, and how your emotions influence you. *Self-awareness,* in turn, allows you to develop an understanding of others, how they perceive you and your attitudes, and how you respond to them in the moment.

The better your self-awareness, the better your self-management, which allows you to develop better interpersonal relationships. To achieve this, it is important to develop positive leadership habits through the regularly review your own performance. In other words, making time to reflect on your performance; by asking for feedback from peers, those that you lead as well as those that follow you; by practicing mindfulness and, finally, by having an honest and critical mentor/coach support you in becoming a self-aware leader.

A useful strategy to implement when you start on you journey of developing self-awareness as a leader is to do a 360° review. During the review, you will ask members of your leadership team to anonymously provide feedback on what they perceive a) your strengths and b) your area for development are. It is extremely important that the questions are answered anonymously and in such a way that your general leadership behaviours become apparent rather than nit-picking specific incidents. It is also important to get at least seven responses to the questions, in order to allow for themes and generalized behaviours to become apparent. Questions that you may consider to include in the review are:

🢒 *Leadership:*

What are the leader's specific leadership strengths?

Provide an example of when you considered the leader to have shown excellent leadership.

How can the leader improve her/his leadership skills?

↪ *Interpersonal relationships:*

When the leader works with people, what interpersonal relationships skills does s/he demonstrate?

Provide an example of when you considered the leader's interpersonal relationships skills to be excellent.

Provide an example of where the leader could have dealt with people differently?

↪ *Motivation:*

Do you consider the leader to be internally or externally motivated?

Provide an example of where the leader demonstrated that s/he is committed to the success of the school.

Provide an example of where the leader experienced difficulties in being motivated.

↪ *Efficiency:*

Provide an example of when the leader's work methods inspired you.

Provide an example of where the leader's work methods could have improved.

Based on the responses from these questions, you can develop an idea of how others see you, which in turn allows you to become mindful of specific behaviour patterns that empowers you when deal with situations, or behaviours on which you should improve.

A second strategy that is worth exploring is to complete a Big 5 personality survey and reflect on the outcome of your strengths and personality traits you should remain mindful of. There are several adequate Big 5 surveys on-line that would be good enough. Or you may approach an educational psychologist to do Big 5 training with you and your leadership team as part of a self-awareness leadership drive. The Big 5 personality traits index looks at how high or low the scores of an individual is on the traits of openness, conscientiousness, extraversion, agreeableness and neuroticism. Considering how high or low you fall on the spectrum of any of the personality traits will give you a better insight on how to approach situations that may either make you feel uncomfortable and where your strengths will allow you to deal well with a specific incident. In addition to your personality traits, it is also important to have a very good understanding of your decision-making style. Depending on whether you make decisions as a design-auditor, flexible, fluent or whether you are avoidant, will help you become a mindful and self-aware leader (more on decision-making styles follow later in the book).

No matter whether you chose to conduct all or any of these tools to develop your self-awareness as a leader, it is important to know that leadership capacity and styles are not fixed, and through becoming aware of which leadership habits you should adjust and which you should maintain and augment, you can improve your leadership style.

Developing Leadership Behaviours

Leadership behaviours are those actions you take in an almost automatic unconscious way. Quite often leaders who have been in the business of education leadership for some time seem to be running on auto-pilot, and what for some of us may seem as innate leadership abilities or personality traits, are actually leadership behaviours that have developed over time. Leadership is not an inborn ability that some people have and some don't. All leadership behaviours are learned behaviours, either through observation or through trial and error. Some leaders have had to learn how to swim in the deep end, and some have been following a deliberate, and planned pathway into leadership. No matter how you ended up on your journey into leadership, there are several behaviours that all leaders, notwithstanding their personality traits or explanatory stiles, have to develop.

The first behaviour is to always exhibit unwarranted optimism. To find (even if it seems impossible) an opportunity in every hurdle, and a benefit in every barrier. You should deliberately and systematically recognize and celebrate small successes amid any less fortunate situation. You should always choose to use praise above punishment and ensure that you maintain regular in-person communication with all members of staff. It is not always easy to look the difficulties in the eye and be honest and authentic about what awaits. It is a fundamental leadership behaviour to be honest and true to who you are. In your communication, learn to be clear, use accessible language, and always make sure you watch the tone and tempo at which you speak. Your tone and body language will always communicate how you feel, be sure that you don't send mixed messages through fake smiles and insincere tone of voice. To paraphrase

Maya Angelou, remember, people may forget what you have said to them or what you have done to them but they will never forget how you have made them feel. Always refer back to the school's vision, when you reflect on you own behaviour as well as when you communicate with others.

The second behaviour is to show tireless energy. This doesn't mean that you should be hanging from the rafters at every opportunity, no does it mean that you should show hyper-active cartoon-like behaviours. However, it does mean that you should never give up. It is hard work to run a successful school and you should always be the person that role models an indefatigable persistence to achieve the vision you have set out. Never giving up, doesn't mean that you don't at times feel despondent. Nor does it mean that you never reflect on your progress or adjust the strategies and priorities you are following to actualize the school's vision. Those are all methods of not giving up.

The third behaviour you should develop is to be courageous. To have courage is to always do the right thing, even if it's not popular. To be courageous is to always stand up for the benefit of your students[1]; to take calculated risks, to ensure that you maintain a moral purpose, and to learn from your mistakes. It takes courage to admit that you have made mistakes, to recognize what those mistakes were and how they influenced those around you as well as the actualization of your vision. It takes courage to start all over again.

---

[1] Standing up for the benefit of students doesn't mean that the students are always right, or that you should choose the student's side above that of a teacher. Sometimes students too must learn how to fail with dignity, and how to stand up, brush themselves off and carry on.

The fourth behaviour is to remain curious, and in a constant state of learnership. You should always be on the look-out for new knowledge, learn about others' experiences and forming an ever-evolving understanding of leadership, education, pedagogy, technology, the human capacity to change as well as teaching, TLA. Being a leader is to never stop learning.

Finally, no leader is an island. Your leadership behaviours should not solely be about you, your successes, power and glory. Effective leadership depends on meaningful collaboration, even with those who you may not like or you may consider to be on the wrong path. If the neighbouring school succeeds at an aspect where you at first thought the strategy would not work, it would be expedient to learn from them, share resources, provide and accept help. It is important to recognise the strengths in others and to serve them with your strengths.

Developing Leadership Potential

Leadership behaviour and skills are not static. You will constantly be in a state of learnership and through your leadership behaviours and habits, you will constantly change. These changes may be in the way you develop your leadership skills, but there may also result in fundamental changes in you as an individual, both professional and private.

The list of qualities you need to develop to reach your leadership potential may include that you:

🔊 Embrace uncertainty.

- ✿ Become Change-able[2]. Change is the only constant in life, there will always be change and one of the most important leadership skills you should develop is to communicate, lead, implement and facilitate change.
- ✿ Become Humble: don't think less of yourself, but rather think of yourself less.
- ✿ Know the strengths and areas of development of your team and your staff, take the time to get to know your people.
- ✿ Develop Trust. Show that you are ready and able to carry out any role, no matter how menial or unpleasant. Join your teachers and support staff in completing less prestigious or tedious tasks. This, in turn, builds trust.
- ✿ Know what motivates and drives your team? What is important to them on a personal level?
- ✿ Use your team's strengths and appoint people to negate their areas for development. Don't spend time trying to fix their areas for development – it is a waste of time and results in demoralised staff, rather empower people who have your weaknesses as their strengths.
- ✿ Run a Dynamic Team. Know who the staff members are to retain and who you should help to move on. You should make it clear that staff members who do not feel comfortable in the culture and climate you are establishing have the right and responsibility to make decisions about their own future at the school, and they either adopt the culture and climate and improve their TLA behaviours or they move on.
- ✿ Become willing to strategically use Human Resources and manage them to achieve your vision. Do not be afraid of moving staff to positions where they will be more effective, and if you have to take the serious step of re-interviewing for

---

[2] To become change-able, you must develop and foster your ability to change.

leadership positions, either internally or from outside, have the courage to do so.

🖙 Be willing and ready to acknowledge when you don't make a difference anymore, or when your vision has expired. Have the courage to know when it is time for you, as leader, to move on yourself.

The Different Functions of Leadership within Your School

Notwithstanding the various leadership or management structures that a principal may wish to implement, there are four core practices and seven mid-level domains of leadership that you should become familiar with. In your journey of becoming an outstanding leader, the attitudes, skills and knowledge you gather in this section will help you focus your knowledge and skills development.

Executive Leadership Practices

There are four categories of core leadership practices that form the foundation of all leaders on all levels: setting directions, developing people, redesigning the organization, and improving the instructional program. Below is a concise but in no means exhaustive list of functions that education leaders engage in.

Setting Directions

🖙 model ethical principles
🖙 building a shared vision
🖙 modelling appropriate values and practices
🖙 fostering the acceptance of group goals
🖙 creating high performance expectations

☞ communicating the direction

Developing People

☞ providing individualised support and consideration
☞ offering intellectual stimulation
☞ modelling appropriate values and practices
☞ keeping track of teachers' professional development needs
☞ planning for, and sometimes providing, on-site professional development
☞ providing mentoring opportunities

Redesigning the Organisation

☞ building collaborative cultures
☞ creating structures and opportunities for teachers to collaborate
☞ evaluating and communicating progress
☞ modifying organisational structures to nurture collaboration
☞ creating structures and opportunities for teachers to collaborate
☞ building productive relations with families and communities
☞ connecting the school to the wider community

Improving the Instructional Program

☞ staffing the instructional program
☞ monitoring progress of students, teachers, and the school
☞ monitoring teachers' work in the classroom
☞ providing instructional support
☞ providing instructional resources and materials
☞ aligning resources

- ☞ focusing the school on goals and expectations for student achievement
- ☞ monitoring teachers' work in the classroom
- ☞ formal classroom observations carried out for teacher evaluation purposes

Middle and Collective Leadership

When you start to think about the specific leadership direction you are interested in, you will notice that one size does not fit all. The established structure within your school may use a different terminology, organisational hierarchy and line management structures, however the follow areas of leadership are more or less universal.

Teaching, Learning and Assessment Leadership

You should have a passion for TLA and an insatiable curiosity to learn about innovative ways of improving student outcomes. Reading about, and doing research on the most effective TLA strategies will become a staple of your daily activity. Most importantly your ability to be communicate areas for improvement in a supportive and empathetic way will be key to your success as a leader. You should have the ability to record, collate and interpret data as well as communicate the findings in a meaningful way.

Safeguarding and Pastoral Leadership

Safeguarding and pastoral leadership requires a strong sense of empathy and patience. You will be working with outside agencies, communicating sensitive information with teachers and driving the inclusive ethos of your school. Time management is one of the most important aspects of your leadership style and a passion for inclusive education is vital for developing your career path in safeguarding and pastoral leadership.

Organisational and Systems Leadership

Your ability to work with data capturing, rational thinking, project management and organising just about anything will be of great use as an organisational and systems leader. Time tables, as well as all the requests and refusals that go hand-in-hand with time tables, exam schedules and exam entries will become part of your day-to-day duties. Do not be surprised if the staff Christmas Party and Prom is directed your way as well.

Resource and Financial Management

Your skills and knowledge of accounting policies and practices, government guidelines and education law will be the bedrock of resource and financial management leadership. You will keep yourself up to date with new funding structures, social mobility grants and corporate support initiatives to bolster the school budget. Meticulous record keeping, transparency and accountability are vital aspects of financial management: there just are no short cuts. Resources include projecting running cost, cash flow, stock keeping, strategic planning, projected growth analyses, staffing cost and planning and implementing strategies to continuously improve inclusive education initiatives, practice and policies. The principles on which the resource and financial management of a school is based are no different than any medium sized business and will take as much knowledge and skill.

Value Added and Experiential Learning Leadership

Some school leaders may consider value added and experiential learning as secondary to the primary task of teaching and learning, however, if you aim to become an outstanding leader, in an outstanding school, this is where you can make a difference. Research into the most current initiatives into teaching and learning, planning and implementing experience-based learning in authentic, real-world settings, communicating with the local community, charities and corporations to develop cooperative learning partnerships will form the basis of your duties. Communicating the value of augmenting the curriculum with staff, parents and other stakeholders is a vital aspect of this leadership role. If project management and seeing the bigger picture, coupled with a creative approach to TLA is your forte, then you will be well suited for this leadership role.

Special Education Needs and Difficulties Leadership

Some principals may wish to combine safeguarding and pastoral leadership with Special Education Needs and Disabilities leadership, however the nature of SEND, investment in time and resources required by both these fundamental aspects of school leadership necessitates that they are separated on both the leadership and implementation level in your school. A passion for educational psychology, secure knowledge of special needs and an appreciation for the complexity of providing inclusive education across all areas of the curriculum is central to becoming a leader in SEND. Within the school you will continuously cooperate with and disseminate sensitive information to all curriculum leaders, TLA leaders, pastoral leaders, financial and resource leaders as well as parents of students with SEND. In addition, you will build strong partnerships with outside agencies and support services on local and national level. This role is time consuming and requires a passion for working towards complete inclusive education.

Continuous Professional Development

The success of any school depends on the quality of teaching and learning. The quality of TLA depends on the quality of continuous development of teachers' skills, knowledge and attitudes. The nature of ever-developing technological advancement requires from teachers to remain at the cutting edge of innovation. If teachers don't use new technology to engage and captivate students, then corporations and social media moguls will. CPD in schools now play a significant role in making sure that TLA stays one step ahead of all the other distractors that are baying for children's attention. In the same way, advancement in knowledge and understanding within the subject areas, new tools and implements as well as new practices and procedures on all levels of leadership, makes this role a signature position in outstanding schools.

Now that you have an overview of the different mid-level leadership roles in a school, it is important that you consider your own interests, strengths and dislikes in order to start designing your journey into leadership, and who you will appoint to each of these essential positions in your school.

Exit Reflection

Leadership in education is a complex and dynamic career that is grounded in selflessness and built on pillars of ethics, morals and values. Leadership in education is not educational management, nor is it a form of social standing that provides unearned adulation. It is democratic, personal and, most of all, it is difficult.

In this chapter, you learned:

- that the concept of school is a uniquely human phenomenon that carries with it an exceptional moral and ethical responsibility;
- the differences between management and leadership in education;
- the various responsibilities of leaders in education;
- the significance of knowing your ethical point of view and clarification of your values;
- how character and attitude makes or undermines your leadership;
- the various functions of leadership in a school.

IV

INCLUSIVE EDUCATION

Inclusive education is concerned with all children and young people in schools: it focuses on the presence, participation and achievement of all students. Inclusion and exclusion are linked together such that inclusion involves the active combatting of exclusive behaviours, and aiming for inclusion is a never-ending process. Thus, an inclusive school is one that is on the move, rather than one that has reached a perfect state. Ainscow

Inclusive education is a question of human rights. The United Nations conventions on the Rights of the Child and Rights of People with Disabilities makes inclusive education an international issue that is central to the everyday practice of all leaders in education. For us to live in fair and democratic societies we need to cultivate inclusivity into every fibre of our schools and communities. The concept of inclusive societies is directly linked to inclusive education.

Why Inclusive Education?

Your school is a microcosm that can become a mirror to society and echo what is happening in its reflection, or it can become a roadmap for society to a future state of existence. In both cases, the moral obligation of holding *the future* of an entire generation of young people in your hands is much larger than you probably anticipated. You will determine the direction a community takes through your actions and attitudes. Do you think this is an overstatement of your influence?

Think about the total number of interpersonal relationships you have fostered, or not fostered, over the span of your career. You have an impact on the knowledge and attitudes of each of those people, and they, in turn, will radiate those beliefs and knowledge as far and wide as their journey may have taken them. In other words, because we all learn through observation, remembering and doing, the attitudes and behaviours that you, as a leader model in your community will become the attitudes and behaviours of the young people that stay behind in your community. Therefore, if you shape inclusive, equality-based, fair and empathetic beliefs, and if you install those attitudes into the students and staff of your school, the energy of those views will eventually become the default setting of the members of your community. And that is how you, through your leadership in your school, can become the driving force of an equal, inclusive community.

The understanding of inclusion and inclusive education is different in every country. In short, we can assert that inclusive education is the right of individuals to achieve self-determination. The right to become competent according to their ability, to form relationships and develop a sense of relatedness in their field of choice and thus develop the autonomy to decide their futures.

To understand why inclusion is such a significant topic, we need to look at the history of inclusivity on a global level. The main driving forces supporting inclusion include the 1994 Salamanca Statement and the United Nations Convention on the Rights of Persons with Disabilities of 2008. These conventions point out that full participation in society of all people, notwithstanding their race, religion, gender or cultural heritage is an absolute human right. However, not all countries have ratified these two conventions which shows the distance education leadership on a global level still has to go. Some matters that need to remain at the forefront of world-wide efforts to improve inclusive societies would include the equal education opportunities of girls in many emerging markets. Another phenomenon that needs attention is the exclusion of young people with albinism in East African nations. Inequality is still rife in post-colonial African nations and the question of LGBTQ rights is all but settled across the globe. I am sure you can look at you own community and see ample examples of where inclusivity still needs to be championed. Further work must be done to promote social justice for minority groups, and recently the inclusion of people with mental health difficulties and disorders as fully integrated members of society, expands the rights people have to equal opportunities in society.

Internationally, the movement towards inclusive education started in the late 1960s and moved like a wave across the globe. For instance, the mainstreaming movements in the USA and

Canada; the Warnock Report of 1978 and Elton Report 1989 in England; the Jomtien World Conference on Education for All, and the Salamanca Statement, all called for *inclusive schooling and support for the development of special needs education.* These conventions came as a reaction to global social-political instability following the second world war. During this time, and amid the Cold War furore, democracy as a construct, became an issue of human rights rather than ideology. The decolonisation of Africa and political independence of the Middle East gained pace, and the social rights movement in the USA all pointed towards the urgency of creating a fair and fully inclusive global society. As the struggle to achieve freedom and equal participation in society developed, it became clear that inclusion is not only a matter of *seeing, accepting* and *promoting* the rights of those left on the periphery of society, but also that those with special education needs and difficulties also have the right to self-determination.

There are three perspectives on the practical im-plementation of inclusive education: *locational integration, social integration* and *functional integration* of learners with special education needs and difficulties (SEND). Such integration policies emphasise assimilating learners into a mainstream environment, providing similar style teaching and learning, but often in separate parts of the school, or a different institution affiliated with the mainstream school. Some difficulties in the effective implementation of integrated practice is that good practice is *seldom widely disseminated,* and *leaders rarely check poor inclusive education practice*s.

The main difference between *integration* and *inclusion* comes down to whether the student is an active partner alongside peers in the learning process, or whether the student is merely present, but mostly overlooked, ignored or *housed* in separate sections of the school. It is not difficult to see that there would be many problems in providing equal education provision where SEND is only integrated and not included in the TLA process. The nature of the SEND usually governs the attitudes towards it. For instance, meeting the needs of children with emotional and behavioural difficulties is considered as being more challenging to integrate into mainstream education that a student with mobility difficulties.

What is even more significant, is that there is a commonly accepted guide for what inclusive education means. A vital aspect of inclusive education is the safeguarding of students with SEND. Schools must identify the needs of students with SEND and ensure they make progress without placing them at risk of injury, bullying or social and academic exclusion. The Centre for Studies on Inclusive Education has published an index for inclusion that encapsulates the ethos of inclusive education. These include:

- ⟡ ingraining inclusive values on all levels of the school;
- ⟡ viewing every life (and death) as of equal worth;
- ⟡ supporting all students and fostering a feeling of worth and belongingness;
- ⟡ increasing full participation of all children, including those with SEND;
- ⟡ reducing exclusion, discrimination, and other barriers to learning;
- ⟡ restructuring school culture, policies and practices to respond to diversity (racial, gender, religious, orientation, non-binary identity and culture) in ways that value everybody equally;
- ⟡ viewing differences as a source of learning and fostering sustained by mutual relationships between the school and its community.

At this point, you have developed an understanding of what inclusion is, what the difference between *inclusion* and *integration* is, and you have probably thought that your biggest challenge as a leader will be to engender inclusive policies and practices in your school. Putting theory into practice has always been one of the most significant challenges faced by education leaders, teachers and support staff. We may look internationally to find examples of other highly considered education systems for different ways of tackling inclusive education. For instance, in Denmark and the United States, inclusive education is approached on a practical level, and is considered more as integration than inclusion. Special classes are placed within the perimeters of the mainstream school, whereas, in the UK, education leaders view inclusive education as providing education to learners with disabilities in age-appropriate general classes, with the needed support to ensure the success of the learner regarding academic, behavioural and social competencies. In South Africa, inclusion takes on a role of social justice and righting the inequities of the past. In India, despite a concerted effort to dispel the shadow of the ancient *caste system*, neonatal developmental problems based on cultural practices, as well as finding an identity as a global leader in its right (despite its strong colonial history), proves to be a significant inclusion challenge. Inclusive education despite its relatively long history, is still in its formative stages, and there is no correct way of doing things. There are, inevitably, many more incorrect ways of doing things.

Inclusion is seen as mainstream education restructuring in such a way that every school can accommodate every child irrespective of disability. A range of assumptions is embodied in the term inclusion, which includes a broader *social and political view*. Inclusive education refers to the process of **increased active participation** of all learners notwithstanding SEND, race, gender, religion and orientation. It also emphasises the restructuring of cultures, policies and practices in all schools to actively encourage the presence and participation of all learners who may be vulnerable to exclusion. Concerning shaping your leadership practice, you should encourage inclusive opportunities and actively encouraging inclusive involvement will be at the forefront of everything you aim to achieve as a leader on every level where you take on a leadership position. Inclusion reaches further than the mere presence of students that are generally excluded based on social, cultural or SEND. Inclusion depends on the changed attitudes of all stakeholders in and outside of the classroom.

The Impact of Policy and Regulatory Frameworks on Inclusive Education

Throughout the world, inclusive education policies follow the central tenets of the rights of the child to equal education and the fundamental right that all humans should have the freedom to actualise their organismic selves. In other words, no-one should stand in the way of a child reaching his/her full potential. It is worth taking a closer look at how a variety of countries approach inclusivity in education, to critically consider and evaluate the policies and practices in your school.

Policy and Regulatory Frameworks Relating to Inclusive Practice

As stated earlier, *inclusive education is directly linked to the idea of an inclusive society*, thus for us to live in fair, democratic nations, we need to cultivate inclusivity into every fibre of our schools and communities. Inclusion is different in every country. In addition, internationally, inclusive practices range from part-time placement in mainstream education to 'reverse integration', where education for mainstream learners is presented in special education classes. In some countries, the use of learning assistants and teachers who are placed, at additional remuneration with learners with SEND is encouraged. Denmark, implements a model of equal quality education in a separate setting. However, with a less homogenous society as previously, it has become clear that the equality of education is has become divided along ethnic and religious lines, and special education sections of schools have as early as 2011, already become holding areas for children from refugee families.

Post-Apartheid South Africa's Education Acts of 1996 and 1998 have set out to provide quality education for all and requires school, *where reasonably practicable* provide education for students with SEND needs in public school. For the most part, the emphasis of inclusive education has fallen on the racial integration of students and staff into previously advantaged communities rather than providing fully inclusive and participating learning opportunities for all students in mainstream education. In South Africa, the importance of high-quality education for all address the question about equality and fairness rather than being an active member of a school through the celebration of differences, the cultivation of empathy, and fostering of fairness.

You should consider your own views on inclusive education and set out a policy that aligns with the ethos and vision of your school. To help you think about how you are going to address the equal and fair provision of teaching, learning and assessment in your school, it is worth looking at the clauses of the Salamanca Statement. The clauses emphasise:

1) the right of every child to education;

2) the uniqueness of each child;
3) the duty of education to respond to the diversity of children through differentiated educational practice;
4) that children with SEN should be accommodated in regular schools with child-centred pedagogy;
5) that schools with inclusive philosophy are the most effective way to deal with discriminative attitudes in society.

In addition to these underlining principles, inclusive education is about *engendering a sense of community and belongingness* and providing an education based on an ethos of inclusion, through a wide-ranging and balanced curriculum that all students can access. It is thus your responsibility as school leader to ensure that your school has systems in place to identify SEND as early as possible and aim to remove all barriers to learning through full participation, with high expectations and suitable targets for all students.

Understanding the Factors which Influence Learning

In schools, we need to create TLA opportunities that include all students. To prepare TLA opportunities that are designed to allow access to learning to all students, you need to form an understanding of the factors that have an effect on inclusive education environments. These factors include social and cultural factors as well as cognitive, physical and sensory difficulties. You will also have to understand how these impact factors will influence your teachers' TLA behaviour, the school budget and additional staffing requirements.

Review Of The Impact Of Personal, Social And Cultural Factors On Learning

Inclusive education plays a significant role in correcting historically exclusive policies and practices, however, it is not limited to only such affirmative endeavours. To understand why inclusion in education is the fulcrum around which inclusive societies are formed, we need to go back to the fundamentals of human nature: the unique, innate human ability to learn. Learning and the young person's access to learning is critical for inclusive education to exist. That's why you need to appreciate how the human learning process works to help you realise how to empower all students. As humans, we learn through observation, retention and imitation. We do not function in isolation, nor do we learn in isolation. When we think about the very act of learning, there are three categories we can distinguish: cognitive, affective and psychomotor development and each one of these categories depend on the environment for a person to fully develop.

From the very foundations of our understanding of what learning is, we see that it never takes place in isolation. Thus, if a young person is excluded from the TLA environment, s/he cannot learn. It is worth looking at some of these theories to see how from the very basic understanding of learning, it always takes place as part of a community. For example, classical conditioning depends on the child learning from stimuli within the environment. An unplanned or natural occurrence (un-conditioned stimulus) provokes an action on the part of the child, which is followed by a consequence based on that action. If the child experiences the consequence as pleasant, then she will behave in a similar way to the stimulus again. If she experiences the consequence as unpleasant, the child will act differently. Over time, this pattern of behaving in a specific way to ensure that the result is pleasant creates patterns of learned (conditioned) behaviour. For instance, if the unconditioned stimulus is going to school and the consequence of going to school is that she is being bullied at school, her natural response will be to feel anxious. Eventually the child will learn that attending school leads to emotions of anxiety, (in other words, school + bullying = anxiety, and ultimately the student will learn that school = anxiety). To avoid the unpleasant feelings of fear and anxiety, the child will stop going to school, and in the same way, she will learn that non-attendance means safety.

If you look at this example through the lens of inclusive education, you can imagine that if the child is the only member of a minority community at your school, and feels isolated at school, she will learn that to stay at home, where she feels welcome, alleviates the stress of isolation. As a result, she will refuse to go to school.

Secondly, operant conditioning explores the impact of rewards and punishers on learning. If a reward/reinforcer is pleasant, the child will continue to behave in a way to ensure that she receives that reward again. If she experiences the result of the behaviour as unpleasant, she will act in such a way to avoid the punishment. Regarding inclusive education, if the child with a learning difficulty volunteers an answer to a maths problem, and is ridiculed by the teacher for getting the problem wrong, the teacher's act of deriding him is experienced as a punishment, and he then learns not to volunteer answers in class.

One of developmental psychology's founders, Piaget, asserts that through a process of assimilation (gathering new information) and accommodation (changing our understanding of old in-formation to accommodate the new knowledge) children go through stages of learning. During any specific stage, the child depends on those people around her to *model* behaviour, for her to assimilate into her understanding of actions and knowledge. If her exposure is to a small repertoire of behaviour and attitudes only, these will be the behaviour and attitudes that she will assimilate into her understanding of the world. However, if her exposure is to a broader, inclusive repertoire of actions, reactions and beliefs, she will have a more expansive, and inclusive view of the world and her place in it.

From these few examples we can see, that from a theoretical perspective, in any case, learning and environment are in-extricably linked. And we can say that even though the ability to learn is innate, learning takes place within and as a result of what happens in the environment. When we ask what happens if any of the personal, social or cultural factors of the environment are withheld form learning, by not including the child in the school or broader community, she will not be able to become a fully developed individual. This is when we see the most persuasive case for inclusive education.

The age of a child plays a significant role in his/her de-velopment. Vygotsky places emphasis on how learning takes place in a zone of proximal development, which necessitates adult support in order for the child to develop beyond his/her *normal independent abilities*. If we remove a child from a situation where an adult can give such support, before the age of establishing such behaviour, it stands to reason that no further development will occur. We see that in situations where severe physical and emotional neglect have taken place, that the developmental stages of these children have not been reached. For example, if a child is excluded from a social environment where the interaction with peers and other significant adults can serve as a stimulus to further development within the zone of proximal development, we see that the child's confidence to participate, make mistakes, adjust behaviour and develop new constructs of understanding is negatively impacted. In the same way if the child is left in isolation from peers and significant other adults to learn, this leads to a plethora of social-developmental inadequacies, such as dearth in self-regulatory development, appreciation of social cues, and advancing positive relationships with peers and teachers. Another example may include the exclusion of a child from a specific learning environment where interaction with peers of a different gender is prohibited. As a result, the ability to communicate with people of the opposite sex will not develop. If these extrinsic barriers remain unattended to, poor-to-fit behaviour will manifest as a barrier to learning.

Environmental factors that influence the development of a child include cultural and religious factors, the educational background of parents and significant adults in the proximity, as well as the socio-economic or financial situation that surrounds the child. It is true that issues within the neighbourhood, such as the prevalence of poverty and low community cohesion, a lack of recreational facilities and inadequate social services, contribute to the exposure to the risk of children and *would decrease resilience rather than strengthen it*. For example, violence in the community, evident poverty and a scarcity of facilities and communal spaces, a lack of healthcare facilities, rejection by peers and peer deviancy, concomitantly increases the influence of social or cultural barriers as risk factors to the optimal development of the child. A nurturing environment is where a child receives exposure to age appropriate and challenging tasks that contribute to her development. It may have an even more detrimental impact on the development of the child if we remove her from that nurturing environment, such as the school, where she can receive the appropriate love and care to bolster her growth. All of these factors have so far been considered in terms of children who have reached age-appropriate developmental stages. When we think about children who present with additional needs for development, we see a stronger case upon which support of inclusive education can be built. In the following paragraphs, we will look at how an inclusive environment bolsters the learning and development of children with Special Education Needs and Difficulties (SEND).

Review of the Impact of Cognitive, Physical and Sensory Difficulties on Learning

For the sake of our understanding of the impact of different cognitive, physical and sensory abilities have on learning, we will need to understand how a few of the most commonly en-countered difficulties of children with SEND impact their ability to learn. The SEND we will look at in this part of the chapter include: Attention Deficit/ Hyperactivity Disorder (ADD/ADHD), Autistic Spectrum Disorder or Conditions (ASD/ASC) Cognitive Develop-mental Disorders (Dyslexia, Dyscalculia, Dysgraphia) as well as neuro-cognitive disorders such as Tourette's Syndrome.

In order for you to model inclusive attitudes such as respect, fairness and diversity, you must have a solid understanding of how different SEND impact on the learning behaviour of students, which in turn will have an impact on the TLA behaviours of staff. If you are not aware of the shared impact of SEND, you will not have all the information you need to make fair decisions about either the teacher or the student's behaviour.

The most encountered and also most controversial of the SEND is Attention Deficit and Hyperactivity Disorder (ADHD). ADHD is a culmination of various biologically based conditions and difficulties that manifests in a persistent pattern of behaviours that cause attention difficulties. Children with ADHD show consistent patterns of inattention (easily distracted and avoids tasks that involves continuous attention), and/or hyperactivity (persistently fidgeting, regularly stand up and wander around) and impulsivity (lash out with no consideration of consequences) which in turn causes a range of difficulties that prevent effective teaching and learning. The child's inability to control the direction of her thoughts when reading a story, causes her to have a lower level of insight into the mechanisms of the text. For example, if she reads about Siobhan's need to be alone and by getting "into the airing cupboard" in *The Curious Incident of the Dog in the Night-Time*, her attention will wander to the airing cupboard which will lead her to think about that time she hid in a cupboard, which in turn will make her think about how her mother reacted, which will remind her of the bread and milk her mother asked her to buy after school. As can be seen in this example, the student cannot keep her focus on Siobhan. She cannot focus on the meaning she is supposed to *derive* (the lesson for the day) form the fact that Siobhan at times want to hide away from people. It is this inability to redirect her attention back to the applicable points during the learning process that leaves the child with ADHD at a disadvantage.

The emotional impact left on the child with ADHD may include a sense of alienation from her peers. She might start to believe that she is not as *clever* as her peers and that may cause a low self-esteem.

There is a raging controversy revolving around ADHD. This is based on the current practice of medicating young people with the condition, as well as several researchers questioning whether the young person's lack of attention and impulse control stems from nurture, rather than a neurological problem. What is important to remember though is, despite the difficulties students with ADHD may face in the classroom, they should not be considered as having a lower cognitive ability than other students.

A second difficulty that has become more identifiable in public forums, is the Autistic Spectrum Disorders or Autistic Spectrum Conditions (ASD/ ASC). ASD are a group of neuro-developmental disorders that include difficulties with reciprocal social behaviour, understanding verbal communication and accessing the correct interpretation of non-verbal communication.

Children that show characteristics of ASD typically favour repetitive, stereotyped activities, fixed patterns or behaviours and are fixated on a narrow band of interests. Children with Asperger Syndrome, a disorder included in ASD, are *typically higher functioning and verbally fluent* yet they show less competence in conversation skills and interpreting intention through the use of body language and other devices that teachers may typically use to manage the learning behaviour in classes. For instance, *the teacher look,* a staple of getting a student to focus on his work again, will be completely lost on the child with Asperger Syndrome. In addition, young people with ASD find figurative language, idiomatic expressions and humour difficult to understand, and will interpret these language devices as literal. This removes the teacher's standard sarcastic retorts of *please, continue talking* from the repertoire of disciplinary devices as well.

These students may act aggressively even when not provoked and will avoid eye contact. They have a general lack of awareness of other people's emotions and feelings. They tend to become obsessed with topics of their own interest and don't have the ability to judge whether it is appropriate to do so at any given time. These difficulties makes the child with ASD prone to bullying and isolation, making school a very unpleasant experience. It is your moral duty to create a climate and culture of understanding and care to completely and actively include these young people.

The child with ASD will typically be one that is misunderstood and if ASD has not been diagnosed could be seen as disruptive (repetitive behaviours), rude (lack of reciprocal social behaviour) or show inattention (stereotyped interests). Therefore, having a child with undiagnosed ASD in your class could disrupt every aspect of TLA, and if your teachers and support staff do not know how to identify or deal with ASD in the class, teaching, learning and assessment will be ineffective at best and disastrous at worst. There are well recorded cases of co-occurrence of ASD and other SEND such as dyslexia and ADHD. Albeit not possible to include all young people with ASD in the mainstream education environment, especially those that are at danger of hurting themselves or others, a significant number of students with ASD can be fully included in the mainstream. In such cases it is your responsibility to ensure that these young people are physically and emotionally safe, free from bullying and able to learn through rigorous train and further development of all teachers and staff.

The exact cause, other than that is a neurological disorder, is not specifically known. And herein lies the controversy. Because we don't know what causes it, we don't know how to treat it. With the advent of blogging and the democratic nature of the Internet, less than scientifically scrupulous publications have placed the causation of ASD at the feet of immunisation against certain childhood illnesses. Such irresponsible publishing has not only contributed to a wave of "disbelievers" but has also placed children at harm of disease because they have not been inoculated.

Cognitive and Developmental Disorders (CDD), albeit not officially placed on a spectrum, may also be seen as a culmination of cognitive and neurological disorders that prevent a child from successful access to the curriculum. CDD include moderate learning difficulties, dyslexia, dyscalculia and dysgraphia. The Latin prefix *dys-* refers to the child's inability to retrieve correct information or access neurological pathways to conduct specific behaviour typical of learning. In the first place, dyslexia is a complex neurological disorder and can cause difficulties with short-term memory, sequencing and information processing. Thus, a child with dyslexia, is for the most part of it, unable to recognise the exact pattern of letters that forms a word. This makes reading (Dyslexia) and spelling (Dysorthographia) more difficult, and without additional support, the student with Dyslexia is at a significant disadvantage in accessing the curriculum. If she cannot read with sufficient speed and accuracy, it means that she will not understand the content, context and specific details of a text to learn from it. It also means that she will find understanding exam questions difficult, and especially where subject-specific terms are similar (such as hypo- and hyper-), she will have to guess what the question requires.

Dyslexia is widely known and yet so many young people suffer from the effects of their reading difficulty. Simple, inexpensive solutions may help keep these students on track, for example installing a voice-activated dictation program on a tablet computer, or making use of existing technology to *read* a text for the student. As leader, it is not your duty to solve these access to the curriculum problems on behalf of your teachers, but rather to set a climate where experimentation and out-of-the-box problem solving skills are encouraged.

Dysgraphia is a writing disorder that renders a child's writing to be distorted. Inappropriately sized and muddled spaced letters, generally illegible writing, inconsistencies in print and unfinished words through omitted letters are typical of this disorder. Dysgraphia slows down responses to questions, and because the child with dysgraphia spends more time trying to write in the correct print, the attention that should be placed on the content of what is written often gets lost. Many teachers will give feedback such as *use better handwriting* or *improve your penmanship* as feedback on a written text, rather than look at the content, knowledge and understanding that *lurks* behind the student's scary script. Clearly, placing emphasis on something that the student has no control over will not lead to continuous improvement of knowledge, skills and attitudes. Again, a simple solution can be found in terms of providing amanuenses during exam time, and the use of tablet computers during lesson time. As leader, your understanding of the provision that is needed will inform the budget of the school, allow you to network with members of the volunteering community to provide the amanuenses or to train staff how to give effective feedback, making actual progress possible.

Dyscalculia is a neurological disorder that looks at the difficulties a child faces in order to understand and manipulate numbers, number sequences and spatial orientation. Children with dyscalculia also find it very difficult to comprehend logical word problems, strategic planning and being on time. Even though dyscalculia is a more persistent problem in mathematics, we associate these behaviours as contributing to many problems elsewhere in school as well. This child will often dress in the wrong uniform, and he will forget his PE kit at home. He will have issues organising his space on the school desk, find it difficult to recognise which steps to follow in a sequence while in the science lab, and more often than not, his homework will show remnants of yesterday's lunch. What makes it even more pervasive is that he will often confuse *left* with *right* and might also get lost on his way to class - which is usually seen by teachers as a poor excuse for tardiness.

A student with dyscalculia may summon scenes from Dante's Inferno in the music room, or score a goal on behalf of the opposing side, during sports lessons, thus causing peer frustration and possible alienation on the playground.

The revelation that poor behaviour might be typical manifestations of a CDD makes it clear that without under-standing the various forms SEND may take, can lead to wide-scale ineffective TLA. In addition to the apparent academic impact of CDD, the social and behavioural problems that go hand-in-hand with these disorders are more a symptom of a neurological disorder. It stands to reason that presenting with typically seen difficulties in behaviours (not remembering homework, problems with keeping the desk tidy and not causing a fire because of a lab experiment that has gone wrong), the child continually faces criticism and reprimand for behaviours over which s/he has very little if any control. It is the teacher's lack of knowledge and understanding, and not the student's SEND that causes difficulties in accessing the curriculum and problems with interpersonal relationships at school.

Finally, physical impairments such as difficulties with mobility, hearing impairments and visual impairments all provide unique barriers to access to the curriculum. Even though physical impairments are easier to see, and therefore teachers are much less likely to mistake the SEND for *bad behaviour*, the social and academic impact of these disorders and difficulties remain severe.

To conclude this section, it is easy to see that the difficulties faced by students with SEND, not only places the child with SEND at an academic disadvantage but it can be socially isolating as well. Together these impact factors paint a rather sad picture of the developmental years for the child with SEND. Therefore, we must conclude that it is only within a fully inclusive TLA environment that children with SEND can develop to the full extent of their abilities.

Suggestions on how to ideally implement inclusive policies and practices into the classroom means that:

- ☞ your school must make reasonable adjustment to include auxiliary aids and services for disabled children, including those with visual, hearing and physical impairments;
- ☞ your students with SEND should be able to reach their own potential in order to achieve their best, and become confident young people that can successfully transition into adult life in order to live fulfilling lives;
- ☞ your teachers should present differentiated TLA opportunities which may include activities on a lower-, middle, and higher ability continuum;

↬ you should use the school budget to provide access to resources for visually impaired students, which may include additional time in preparation to print enlarged text, or the use of technology such as audio-visual devices or software. This might mean that teachers spend time to learn how to use (and troubleshoot) these devices;

↬ you should be aware of new technology and pedagogy that empower teachers and parents of SEND students to work closely together to provide access to the curriculum to students with SEND;

↬ you set the tone and example for attitudes and practices that promote inclusive education in your school.

Schools that emphasise inclusive practices benefit all students, not only those with SEND. Because everybody learns in their way and in their own time, implementing differentiated lessons through a wide range of learning modalities benefits not only the students with SEND but also those who are either more able to learn through visual or auditory stimuli; respect for diversity creates a climate where all students can be safe and welcome, as well as provide an environment where full access to the curriculum is available to all students, not leaving any child behind whether they have SEND or not.

Applied Leadership and Inclusion

To be able to ensure that inclusion becomes an integrated part of the school's way of doing things, teachers and support staff should have the opportunity to identify their areas for de-velopment regarding their knowledge and practice of inclusive education strategies. The opportunity should be given to them to participate in CPD and the opportunity share their good practice with staff at both a formal and informal level should actively be encouraged. As you develop your vision for a fully inclusive school , you may want to add Inclusive Practices as a permanent point on meeting agendas from administrative, custodial, support and department level to whole school meetings as well as meetings with parents and governors.

The Teacher's Role and Responsibilities Relating to Inclusive Education Practice

Leaders in education must ensure an inclusive approach to school management which translates into providing all learners, including those with SEND, access to equal education and educational resources at mainstream schools and to allow them to learn from the same curriculum as other students. However, inclusion is not only the concern of educators tasked with teaching learners with SEND; it includes all stakeholders in the school including leaders, teachers, students, parents and service providers.

All stakeholders should be held accountable for fostering a culture of inclusive education, developing inclusive values and beliefs and meaningful, relevant TLA opportunities. Most pointedly, classroom teachers are directly accountable for the progress and achievement of all students in their class, and this includes those with SEND. It is the teacher's role and responsibility to provide effective differentiated learning opportunities, as well as her responsibility to review her TLA behaviour and adjust where it falls short of the high expectations we hold for all students and staff. And, as you hold a clear expectation of high-quality TLA through differentiated work and inclusive learning practices, your teacher must hold high-quality effort, commitment resilience and a positive attitude form all students, including those with SEND.

It is the responsibility of leadership to regularly review the quality of teaching for all students and where necessary, improve teachers' understanding of SEND and appropriate strategies to use in class. One way that you can use your budget to ensure that SEND provision is continuously improving is to employ a Special Education Needs and Difficulties Coordinator (SENDCo). The main aim of having a SENDCo is to help identify SEND, coordinate support strategies and record and evaluation provision as well as encourage subject teachers to develop their awareness of SEND through specific knowledge and skills that will help to set up an inclusive classroom environment. Some of the duties of the SENDCo may include:

- overseeing and coordinating the day-to-day operation and implementation of the school's SEND policy;
- liaising with specific teachers and outside agencies relevant to children that are in social care or looked after, at risk of adversity or has SEND;
- providing advice on the use of the schools designated budget aimed at SEND provision and progress;
- liaising with parents of students with SEND and ensuring that both the school and the parents are at all times well informed of incidents, diagnoses and progress;
- acting as key point of contact for outside support agencies;
- liaising with education and support providers to ensure a smooth transition onto the phase of the student's education or support;
- ensuring that the school keeps the records of all SEND students up to date.

The school should ensure that the SENDCo has sufficient time and resources to carry out the required functions. As leader, you should promote inclusive practice, first and foremost, by modelling inclusive behaviour. Inclusion should not be seen as an additional aspect or feature of your school, but rather the fulcrum around which your entire ethos is developed. Even though we have placed specific emphasis on students with SEND and students that are at risk of adversity, in care or of particular safeguarding concern, it is essential that all students benefit from an inclusive educational environment.

How to Create and Maintain an Inclusive Learning Environment

You may lift your eyebrows at this point in despair because there isn't even money for keeping class sizes manageable, much less for ensuring individual attention. Keep in mind that you have an entire school community out there that can be harnessed to help. Instead of paying for additional teaching staff, you may wish to make use of trainee teachers to gain experience on an ad hoc basis: such as done for sports coaching, why not remedial TLA provision. You may ask for support from parents and instead of paying for an additional staff member to do the one-on-one remedial lessons, have your SENDCo train parents in safeguarding, remedial reading, writing and mental arithmetic skills.

Another strategy may be to reshuffle extramural duties. Have parents and members of the grandparent community do duty on the playground, or coach the second and third sports teams or play the piano as choir practice. Such participation by parents and community volunteers will free teachers to spend more time planning for inclusive lessons, emphasise more specialist remedial or inclusive education initiatives or engage in training to improve their inclusive education practice.

Points of Referral Available to Meet Individual Learning Needs

It is the school's responsibility to continuously assess whether students are in need of additional moral, spiritual or SEND support. You may wish to include the one-on-one tutorial and mentoring session, where each student has the opportunity to discuss their progress with a teacher or support staff. These meetings once a term will create a waypoint for the identification of SEND in students that are not showing appropriate progress towards their target. Support staff should report these concerns to the SENDCo. Again, despite the fact that such mentoring is aimed at sustaining an inclusive environment, all students will benefit from such a mentoring strategy. Continuous liaison and relationship building with outside agencies or in cases where there are no government sanctioned agencies, with professionals in private practice such as Child and Adolescent Mental Health Services, Educational Psychologists, Social Services and Police services.

In your school, you should have a system that can identify and communicate inclusive education needs with teachers and support staff. You should provide person-specific guidelines for supporting each child with inclusive education or SEND needs.

There are four classifications that can be made when referral to the SENDCo has been made. The first is *marginal groups* according to race, religion, gender, cultural heritage or identifying as LGBTQ. Monitoring and supporting fully inclusive TLA participation is essential to ensure these students make efficient and sufficient progress.

The second is when *insufficient progress* has been identified and the school has either identified emerging SEND or other inclusive needs. The school should include these students' names to a specific focus group list in order to keep a closer eye on their progress, communicate their needs to staff and provide individualised support. This means that the school has to recognise the need for additional support and an individual support plan (ISP) should be designed, disseminated to teachers and in-class support staff, implemented and should be actively monitored on an ongoing basis by both the SENDCo and class and whole school inspections. Examples of such focus groups may include students who have mild cognitive difficulties (MCD), or students that are at risk of adversity (poverty, neglect, physical, emotional sexual abuse, parent criminality or mental health difficulties, students that take care of parents or siblings, children living with HIV/AIDS).

A third classification is when a student has had a formal assessment of *special education needs* and the student has received a statement/diagnosis of SEND. A document with the specific needs and extra support guidance should be issued by the Educational Psychologist. It also means that additional funding from the school budget should be allocated to provide specialist, individual support within the school. The specialist support may include remedial one-on-one or small group sessions, additional support staff to help in the classroom, the physical adjustment of the facilities, and access to the curriculum through ICT solutions.

Finally, a student may have been recorded as having *moderate learning difficulties*, which implies a lower cognitive ability that warrants additional support in class. In addition to the support provided by auxiliary staff in the classroom, as well as the support from the SENDCo, peer learning activities such as group work, experiential learning (where the student spends time in a real-world setting gaining experience and confidence), or counselling from outside agencies as coordinated by the SENDCo.

Ways to Promote Equality and Value Diversity

The first way of promoting equality is by keeping reliable and valid data on the progress of students with SEND and inclusive education needs. Through this use of data, school leaders can determine if they are efficiently providing support, differentiation and inclusive opportunities, and where they have noticed a shortfall, they should actively invest in improving provision. The school should record provision and how impactful these arrangements are. How the quality of differentiated teaching contributes to the progress of all students with SEND over time. The information regarding the needs and academic progress should be compared to national averages for similar SEND to measure their effectiveness in inclusive education practice.

Ways to Promote Inclusion

The frontline of inclusive education provision is in the classroom. The culture and climate, regarding inclusive ethos and practice, that is set by the teacher will be adopted by the students in their everyday lives. One of the most significant ways of ensuring an inclusive classroom is to create a culture of acceptance, empathy and supportive participation. For example, students with ASD often become victims of bullying, and usually in ways that are not explicitly apparent. A word, which may seem innocuous in any other context, can become a tool for discrimination against the child with Asperger's. Being highly sensitive to such covert attempts at discrimination and bullying, and being relentless in addressing such issues is essential to establish an inclusive culture in the classroom. It is also necessary to recognise and celebrate all academic progress. A clear reward system, to highlight students' work, and celebrate academic progress toward their specific target, will allow all students to see that everybody can and must make progress. It is crucial that the teacher models inclusive practice by not unfairly rewarding students with SEND if they have not made progress towards the target. Undue rewards will prove to your students that minimum effort is required from him/her. It might also be seen as favouritism, and may even lead to bullying. Also, the student with SEND may stop working towards her goal, which goes against the high expectations that you hold for all students including those with SEND.

Exit Reflection

Critical views on inclusion involve concerns that inclusion places a "disproportionate influence on the education system" and that the burden on limited financial resources is unsustainable. Further concerns include the ability of teachers in mainstream education to provide full participation and quality education based on a *lack of training, ignorance about specific disabilities* as well as *an unwillingness to accommodate students.* There is a debate whether the existence of alternative providers such as Learning Support Classes (in schools) and special needs schools that function independently, subscribe to the understanding of what inclusion actually is. Some feel that inclusive education is forced upon parents with SEND children and that often the ideological basis for inclusion overrides the what might be more practical or what is more beneficial for the individual child. Examples given by opposing voices include that there is lack of flexibility in the curriculum and that the classroom environment hampers inclusive education. They suggest that a special education environment may be more suited to cater to the needs of children. There are also calls that specialist educators are best equipped to provide special education for learners with SEND. If this is true, you may ask if these views stem from genuine inclusive practices or rather from a perspective of integration.

By thinking about the facts as mentioned above, perceptions, examples and criticisms, you will be able to form your philosophy of inclusive education and how you will use the school or department budget to support inclusive education initiatives.

As an education leader, you have to ask yourself:

1) How do I communicate the need for increased inclusive practices?
2) What are the current assumptions and views of the students, staff and school community regarding inclusive education?
3) How effective is the inclusive education practice in my school or my department?
4) What must I do to improve the inclusive education practice of everybody in the school?

V

LEADERSHIP STYLES

Leadership in education is not easy. As a leader in your school, you are accountable for the successful functioning of a complex organisation in one of the most essential service industries of our times. Not only do you have the responsibility to maintain a calm and positive culture and climate for the day-to-day running of the school, but you also have the moral imperative of *in loco parentis* (in the place of the parent) which places an additional dimension of leadership at the heart of your school. This is an obligation that no CEO or managing director of a corporate service provider has to face. You carry the weight of taking on the responsibility for the actions and behaviours of all the stakeholders in your school that drive the cognitive, behavioural, social-emotional, moral and ethical development of every single child, and in some cases, you do this at the same or even higher commitment as that of a parent. You are accountable, above and beyond the day-to-day management of an organisation that facilitates the development of the knowledge, skills and attitudes that are essential to sustain continued growth and development of entire communities. I believe the weight of these responsibilities places education leadership in a league of leadership beyond that of any Fortune 500 company. You may think that this statement sounds a bit over the top, but if you carefully consider the lives you are accountable for, on a daily basis, you will probably agree.

Even though leadership as an organizational function and human phenomenon has been researched to a great extent, the very dynamic and complex nature of leadership in education has yet to be developed. This lack of the specific understanding of what it means to be a school leader has contributed to attempts of academia and politicians to superimpose models of leadership suitable to corporate settings onto the education environment. This has given rise to exorbitant requirements for paperwork, increased stress levels and less that effective TLA outcomes.

Purposeful Leadership

In order for you to develop your leadership skills you must build on your knowledge and understanding of the values and ethics of leadership in school. You must explore and develop your *fit-for-purpose* approach to leadership that encourages and enables excellence in teaching and learning. You must also learn about the various leadership styles that exist and the benefits and barriers each of those styles encompass. You must learn how to discern which style of leadership fits your personality and the culture of your school best as well as how to use the different leadership styles to achieve the best results. Learning how leadership has a moral and ethical imperative as well as how trust forms a cornerstone of your role in the school, will help you develop an understanding of leadership pitfalls and how to avoid them.

Conflict as a Factor in 21st Century Leadership in Education

Leadership in the 21st century is characterised by conflict, and you are faced with managing all aspects of this conflict as a critical part of your duties as a leader. Amid all of the voices calling for change, for improvement and greater accountability, it remains your responsibility to create an environment that is suitable for effective TLA take place, and therefore, you must develop a style of leadership that will empower your teachers to become the outstanding practitioners that they can be.

Conflict between Quality and Quantity of Teaching, Learning and Assessment

You will face the constant pressure of quality of TLA versus the quantity of outcomes that need to be completed as directed by the National Curriculum. The pace at which schools must function is often mind-boggling, and the role a leader in modern education plays is not only to keep track of the daily tasks of teaching, learning and assessment (TLA) but also to actively participate in spearheading growth and improvement of the school. The pace at which students are expected to learn and the sheer amount of work teachers have to complete creates a conflict between stimulating curiosity in the student, establishing a growth and progress-based mind-set and getting the job done. This makes your role as leader a complex one. Furthermore, a contributing factor to the complexity of your role is the extent in which ambiguity and conflicting ideas increases through political pressures and interventions that want to see results in an unrealistic time frame.

Your work as a leader in education has become much less predictable and less structured which contributes to the conflict between quality and quantity of learning outcomes. You have accountability for continuous improvement of TLA despite the whirlpool of constant changes that go hand-in-hand with economic crises, political changes, fundamental changes in the identity and ideology of societies. This is augmented by increasing expectations from industry and higher education institutions that insist that students are *completely formed* and *action-ready* by the time they enter higher education or the work place. In addition to these changes, there is also an increased emphasis on inclusion of minority groups, gender and racial equality as well as social mobility of less advantaged sectors of society.

Conflict Arising Due to Technological Advancement

With the advent of mobile technology, there has also emerged a conflict between traditional views on pedagogy and evolving approaches to teaching and learning. The battle concerning a balanced attitude towards blending old and new methods of TLA and an all-in approach to new technology is probably the most significant conflict you will have to manage as a leader. The technological tectonic plates have been shifting at a pace last witnessed with the advent of the Model T Ford, but this time technology is growing at an exponential pace. Within a few months existing technology will be outmoded, and young people's appetite for novel and innovative learning tools increase at a similar pace as the advancement of new technology. Thus, finding a balance between financial investment in technology and employing time-honoured methods of TLA causes the most significant conflict in education leadership. In the same manner, data management tools, teacher training and prescribed procedural maps are as dynamic and ambiguous as emerging teaching technologies.

Conflict Due to Increased Accountability Requirements

There is often a conflict between expectations from how and what governments want to see in the reporting on academic progress, school improvement, financial governance, social mobility and the change in attitudes towards inclusive, non-discriminatory practices as well as the expectations of parents and other stakeholders. These expectations want to superimpose a rigid and formally structured corporate identity on the phenomenon of teaching and learning, which by definition is fluid and flexible. Students are seen as the primary client of the school, and changes towards the institutional attitudes and approaches to TLA, student voice and the rights of students often cause a sense of conflict within educator ranks. Each teacher is accountable for the progress of every student, and based on our understanding that not everybody learns at the same pace and in the same way, there is conflict between the requirements and learning needs of the individual student versus that of the collective. The amount of paperwork and administrative box-ticking that is characteristic of modern education, as well as accountability structures and requirements, this relegates school leaders to exclusively managerial roles, which in turn is an enormous waste of a potential resource for TLA improvement.

Conflict Due to Time as a Limited Resource

There is an ongoing conflict between ring-fencing time for teachers to continuously assess the progress, learning and support-needs of students as well as time to develop new resources and professional development. In the same way, leaders need time to build professional relationships with teachers, students, as well as the broader education community, yet they are expected to be accountable for myriad administrative duties. There remains a critical assumption that teaching, learning and assessment will improve if leaders provide detailed feedback to teachers that include suggestions for change. However, leaders must have the time, the knowledge, and the consultative skills to give their teachers valid and useful advice about their TLA practices. Teachers must have the time to reflect on advice, plan new lessons based on feedback and implement the changes that were suggested. One of the most widespread complaints of teachers is that leaders do not have a relevant understanding of the subject matter, the specific methods of instruction and even developmental level of the students to be able to make appropriate and useful comments. Therefore, the conflict between available time to be a thoughtful leader and being a successful leader contribute to how you will develop your fit-for-purpose leadership style.

Approaches to Leadership

To navigate your way through these conflicts and the needs of your students and staff, is no mean feat. In order to ensure that your leadership approach, method and style doesn't contribute to another layer of conflict within your school, it is imperative for you to know the most appropriate leadership approaches and methods as well as the leadership style that suits your personality bests

A Matter of Control

Leadership and control are often considered to be synonymous. There is no doubt that one aspect of leadership involves control. Yet too often, control is comparable with power, and that in the modern education environment is a toxic inaccuracy. We can spend substantial time debating the concept of authority in education leadership. How much control is too much control? And once you have decided how much power you should have, there is the question of how much we should depend on human agency? How much should students or teachers depend on their locus of control to fulfil their tasks? For example, as a classroom teacher, you may often consider control to be the way you manage the behaviour of your class, and during classroom observations, teachers are usually rated as good or bad based on such control. However, you may insist that to empower your students to manage their own behaviour. It is more important that learning behaviour is dynamic and that a one-size-fits-all type of control over students is counterproductive. In the same way, you may think that it is expected of you as leader, to either manage, or empower the teachers that are under your "control".

Leadership theorists and Gurus, Robert Tannenbaum and Warren H. Schmidt , have identified four different control modes or approaches to leadership: Autocratic (your influence rises with the hierarchical level of your role) Democratic (higher levels of influence attributed to those in hierarchically lower levels or roles) Anarchic (relatively little influence by any level or role) Polyarchic (high levels of influence by all levels or roles). In modern education, there is a tendency to lean towards a democratic control mode. This is significant because the control mode that is predominant in the leadership structures, will inevitably become the control mode that is followed in class, as well as the wider culture of the school. It is important for you as leader to have an understanding of your own preferred mode of control and how that influence the other members of the leadership team.

Leadership Models

Leadership models look at what types of leadership be-haviour you will employ in order to achieve the most effective TLA environment. Leadership behaviour includes a high level of supervision - during which you will give directives and intensely monitor progress. There is mid-level supervision - during which you will provide emotional support and encouragement, and you will have to encourage enthusiasm. And, a low-level of guidance expects from you as a leader to withdraw your direct supervision to promote the development of an internal locus of control, in which the leadership behaviour is only to provide direction. The latter of the three is the riskiest strategy and should be considered in an established culture and climate based of earned trust and shared vision of mastery of all aspects of TLA.

Contingent Leadership

The model of contingent leadership places emphasis on the situation you find yourself in. Your relationships and leadership behaviour will depend on the specific tasks each of your teachers have to engage in and complete. Contingent leadership is a two-dimensional model that is task oriented and provides little room for allowing follower growth and input. According to this model, you must match your leadership style and behaviour to your settings. Contingent is often used in crisis situations or when you have to implement urgent and wide ranging school improvement changes. Leaders that take charge of failing schools, or schools where student or teacher behaviour is an impediment to effective TLA will use contingent leadership to establish a new vision and behavioural expectations.

Participative Leadership

Participative leadership encourages leadership behaviour that invites contributions from teachers, students and parents on all levels in all school decisions. This includes policy and practices in teaching and learning, the use of technology as well as practical issues such as playground supervision and taking responsibility for developing an inclusive school culture. You will give stakeholders relevant information regarding school issues, and a majority vote will determine the course of action the school will take. It provides your teachers and students with the opportunity to be active participants in shaping not only the future success of the school, but also take more responsibility for their achievement. Participative leadership empowers teachers, students and parents to use their own creativity to develop more effective TLA processes and determine the work ethic and culture of the school.

One of the outcomes of a participative model of leadership is that teacher and student morale remains high because they appreciate the chance to be part of the school's decision-making process. Even more so, because teachers, students and parents are given the prospect to develop a personal stake in the success of the school, they have the chance to lead necessary change.

Participative leadership is often a slower form of decision-making, however, the advantages it holds may make this the appropriate leadership model for your school. You must think about your preferred mode of control before you consider this model of leadership. For example, if you prefer an autocratic mode of control, this will be in conflict with a participative leadership model.

Transformational Leadership

Transformational leadership is a leadership model that facilitates change in social systems such as schools. If it is well implemented, transformational leadership creates valuable and positive change in the teachers, students and parents with the end goal of empowering all stakeholders to become emergent leaders. It increases the motivation, morale and performance of stakeholders by including a sense of identity and self in the shared vision. Such a leader encourages a collective character of the school, and they do this by being a role model that inspires teachers and support staff. You can challenge your team to take more significant ownership of their work, and through understanding their strengths and areas for development, you can empower teachers and students, to participate in activities and responsibilities that increase their performance. A polyarchic mode of control is best suited for transformational model of leadership.

Situational Leadership

The situational leadership model looks at how you use your influence over your colleagues and at the nature of leader-follower relations. It emphasizes how you communicate the shared vision; how you convey high performance expectations; how you project self-confidence, and modelling appropriate behaviour; as well as how you express confidence in followers' ability to achieve the collective purpose. In the situational leadership model, your leadership behaviour is determined by the level of competence and the support needed by the teacher. If the teacher's knowledge and proficiency is low, the leadership behaviour will necessitate a high level of supervision and coaching. Conversely, if the teacher's knowledge and skill is high, the leadership behaviour will allow more independence. If you choose a situational leadership model you must also consider the way in which you provide emotional support to the various stakeholders.

The teacher's level of skills and knowledge will determine how much emotional support is needed. As the teacher's proficiency develops, the level of emotional support will change. A strength of the situational model is that you are encouraged to consider a range of appropriate leadership behaviours and adjust them as you deem appropriate. Flexibility in your approach is key to the success of achieving your leadership objectives. In short, according to situational leadership, your leadership behaviour is delivering the correct amount of supervision (directing behaviour) and arousal (supporting behaviour) in order to produces the best learning and developmental environment for TLA to be effective.

Choosing A Leadership Model

Applying the right leadership model in your school depends on what your vision and desired outcomes are. By aligning your leadership behaviour with your vision and strategic goals, you can focus more on the leadership model that make the most sense for your school. For example, if you need to quickly change the TLA practices or way in which progress is measured and reported due to improvements in technology, or new directives from the local authority, you may want to focus on the contingency and transformational leadership models. If you are in a consolidation phase of change and your vision is to create a democratic culture where shared ownership of TLA empowers teachers and students to develop their own internal locus of control, you may consider the situational model of leadership. Whereas a participative model of leadership will be useful once consolidation of changed policy and practice has taken place and further areas for development are identified and considered for change.

Types of Leadership Styles

Leaders are not born. Leaders are not made. Leaders are not crowned. Leadership is not accidental. Leadership is a deliberate set of behaviour and consideration based on knowledge and practised skills. The amount of time and critical thinking you put into actively improving your leadership skills will make or break your leadership bid. It is during this time of personal growth that the success of your school is determined.

Much too often school leaders rush in where angels fear to tread, because they depend on their personality traits to sustain their leadership behaviours. In many cases enthusiastic teachers find themselves pushed into a position of leadership. This is often done without any consideration of training, personal goals or capacity and then when either the teacher burns out, or their leadership skills fail to make an impact, the blame for their failure is attributed to the teacher's temperament or leadership ability.

Once you have decided that you will endeavour into the world of education leadership, your first step will be to become knowledgeable of, and then choosing, a leadership model. Your choice of the model that would be most fit-for-purpose to your school, should not be a haphazard activity. You should consider the most appropriate leadership style for you, your teachers and the extent of the necessary school improvement that you will have to drive.

There are several authors that have contributed to our understanding of leadership styles. Many of the more recent theories on leadership style make use of a combination of existing leadership styles to show how you can use your leadership style to become a fit-for-purpose leader in a wide range of settings. Because you are in charge of considering and deciding on your style, I provide you with a baseline of leadership styles, of which you can create a medley that is suitable for your school and situation.

The Charismatic Leader

The charismatic leader is seen as a person who holds certain character traits that imbues trust, obedience and a certain level of achievement. Her leadership behaviour encourages followers to feel that she identifies with them, and her confidence speaks of success. She is often considered to be a "visionary" leader, one that can convince teachers and students to believe in an appealing and believable future state, which in turn enthuses stakeholders to help her to achieve it. We may differentiate between two kinds of charismatic leaders. The first is personalised in which characteristics include self-aggrandising, exploitative, authoritarian leadership behaviours. The second is socialised which is known for altruistic, collectively oriented, egalitarian leadership behaviours.

The benefits of adopting a charismatic leadership style is that leaders who have demonstrated more charismatic behaviours managed to increase the cohesiveness of their teams which in turn resulted in improved team performance. However, there are critical disadvantages in sustaining outcomes that were achieved based on the charisma of a leader. The over-reliance of students and staff on the leader may result in the form of learned helplessness and social loafing among teachers. When teachers and student become too dependent on the direction and directives of the leader, they do not employ their own creative and critical faculties. Moreover, charisma alone is not enough. In order to make a successful and quality school leader.

As charismatic leader, you must hold the best intentions of the school and school community at heart yet without cultivating other leadership qualities to support your charisma, you may find that you become overburdened and you could even face burnout.

Another disadvantage of choosing a charismatic leadership style is that you may have difficulty in turning over control to others because you enjoy having the power, or you don't feel that anyone else in the school can handle the duties in the same way as you can, resulting in unsustainable leadership practices.

The Transformational Leader

The transformational leader is considered to be able to motivate teachers and students to look at their work from different angles. She is aware of her team's goals and she is able to help them adjust their goals to be compatible to the school's shared vision. She is able to inspire and empower her team to attain higher levels in the outcomes and achievement of students; and she looks beyond her own interests towards those of the school community at large. As transformational leader, you will hold the following four transformational characteristics.

Idealised influence—you exhibit high levels of integrity and you provide a strong sense of the direction, and you articulate an exciting vision. This may result in you being admired and respected in such a way that teachers and students wish to emulate you.

Inspirational motivation—you communicate and have positive, high expectations of teachers and students, and this in turn motivates and inspires the people around you. You help to provide meaning, optimism, and enthusiasm in order to achieve the school's shared vision.

Intellectual stimulation—you encourage teachers and students to develop their critical thinking skills, to challenge assumptions and beliefs they hold. You reframe problems in such a way that the opportunities rather than the difficulties shine through and you view problem-solving as an opportunity to look at old solutions in new ways.

Individualissed consideration— you pay attention to teachers' and students' needs and aspirations and you actively develop the potential of each teacher and student by creating new opportunities for growth through CPD, coaching and mentoring.

As a transformational leader, you will genuinely believe in your vision and in the "rightness" and benefits of what you want to achieve. The selling of your vision never stops. Your teachers and students receive continuous encouragement and reinforcement to be an active part of working towards actualising the vision. However, be careful, because any sign that you may be manipulating your teachers and students, or that you may have a hidden agenda, it will destroy the trust that is necessary for this style of leadership to be effective. If your teachers and students see the vision itself as insignificant, or there is a mismatch between your vision and their beliefs and needs, you may have a rebellion on your hands.

A leader who fails to communicate will probably fail. You must continuously provide feedback on progress, keeping in mind that enthusiasm can very quickly seem synthetic and that you should anchor the mainstay of your leadership style on trust. The transformational leadership style places individual stakeholder's contributions and needs as a priority. The down side could be that teachers and students often begin to feel used, that they feel they are only cogs in a machine and that their work is not essential. This feeling makes them lose interest.

The Transactional Leader

Transactional leadership behaviours are less personal and based on a detached exchange relationship between the leader and teachers. This leader provides quid pro quo in return for specified TLA behaviours. The exchange of remuneration for specific behaviours involves monitoring performance according to clear and concise structures and performance indicators. They only provide intervention and support when they consider it appropriate, and only if problems become evident correction is required. As a transactional leader, you will base performance of teachers and students on the type of short-term goals that make it easy for them to do their work. Rewards and punishment are used as motivators (the desired follower actions are rewarded, while disapproved actions are punished) in order for teachers and students to do their tasks in the shortest possible time to receive incentives, whether monetary or psychological. This is a rigid leadership style and does not allow flexibility or adjusting prescribed practices. It seldom allows for listening to suggestions from teachers and students and this style does not encourage critical and creative thinking. The has been an international tendency, specifically in the United Kingdom and education systems in the far east, to favour a transactional leadership style. The jury is still out on how effective this will prove to be. However, if the current trends in recruitment and retention in the UK are considered, it seems that transactional leadership is not very popular among teachers.

The Laissez Faire Leader

The Laissez-faire leader holds an attitude of letting things take their course, without intervention or explicit support. With this style of leadership, we see that leaders delegate duties in an indifferent and even lax, hands-off approach. This approach allows teachers and students to make the decisions in their own way and it is serendipitous if their style happens to align with the vision of the school. In general, *Laissez Faire leaders* are less efficient, and this leadership style results in the lowest productivity among teachers and students.

The Ethical Leader

The ethical leader, much like the transformational leader, acts for the greater good of the school community. The ethical leader places *the good* of teachers, students and parents over her self-interest and is often related to as the *leader as servant* (altruism). As an ethical leader, you are characterised as caring, honest and empathetic, and your decisions are based on fairness. In your communication, you frequently refer to ethical standards and when you use rewards and punishments, which is more considered to be a transactional approach, you are fair and consider what would be ethical rather than what is prescribed by policies and procedures. Importantly, your behaviour is in line with the views you champion. We find three distinct character traits in the ethical leader:

1) fairness—acting fairly and honestly;

2) power-sharing—listening to stakeholders' ideas and opinions as well as allowing them to be involved in decision-making concerning their targets and goals, and;

3) role clarification—clearly communicating and clarifying the expectations, responsibilities, accountability and specific roles of all the stakeholders.

As an ethical leader, you will be people-orientated and behave with the utmost integrity, towards your staff. You will provide and follow moral guidance; you will adhere to the mantra of *praise in public and punish in private*; and you will be concerned with the sustainability of high outcomes through continuously improving teaching and learning.

The Authentic Leader

Authentic leadership suggests a genuine kind of leadership: the type of leadership that one may consider to be natural or instilled since a young age. This leader has an optimistic temperament and is seen as hopeful, open-ended, visionary and creative. The authentic leader responds to social circumstances and the need for improvement and change in a values-informed way.

As an authentic leader, you have a sophisticated, knowledge-based, and skilful approach to leadership. You acknowledge and accommodate the genuine needs of teachers, students, parents and broad community in an integrative way. You approach administration and procedures in a way that makes sense and add value to TLA rather than adhere to prescribed processes that are cumbersome and arrests the progress of students.

As an authentic leader, you share some characteristics with the ethical leader: most importantly that of altruism and a significant internal moral imperative. Your typical leadership behaviour makes use of and encourages competencies based on Positive Psychology to foster a positive ethical climate. You will practise and promote self-awareness, empathy, developing an internal locus of control and transparency. Some of the most critical leadership behaviours you will show are openness and clarity in the way you interact with stakeholders. This will include sharing information, keeping safeguarding issues in mind, making collaborative decisions, and providing constructive, positive feedback. In the same way, as with the ethical leader, the mantra of *praise in public and punish in private* is essential.

Dr Jacques Mostert

Distributed Leaderships

Schools are organic organisations and any attempt to superimpose rigid leadership models on a school may be met with resistance. That being said, a distributed model of leadership can be moulded to be effective in a school environment. Unlike, models of leadership that depend on individuals that take on a leadership role and occupy a position of leadership, we base the concept of distributed leadership on the tenet that leadership in a school is a fluid and emergent process. Different members of a group, depending on their expertise and skills, will steer the process of leadership. Leadership is delegated to different people at various levels of the school to fulfil different roles.

The best way to describe distributed leadership is by giving an example: in Flagship Secondary School all the members of staff have responsibility for TLA of at least one class, including the principal. During curriculum meetings, the curriculum leader of English takes on the leadership role and his followers includes the principal who, herself, takes three English classes per week. At this meeting, she follows the direction and directive of the Curriculum Leader of English, whereas, during whole school meetings, the Curriculum Leader of English is subordinate to the principal. In the same way, the lead teacher for inclusion may call a meeting during which both the Principal and the Curriculum leader of English are subordinates. Therefore, our understanding of distributed leadership moves the study of characteristics and leadership behaviour of formal leadership roles to an understanding of how shared multi-level, interactive leadership practices work on all levels of the school structure.

There are three characteristics of distributed leadership:

- ☞ *leadership as a social process* — an activity that takes place in and through the interpersonal relationships and networks of influence in the school, rather than formal hierarchy.
- ☞ *leadership as an outcome*— leadership results in the learning and growing of all stakeholders in the school and depends on the ability of a variety of individuals to create a climate and culture where new knowledge, skills and attitudes are directly aimed at the positive outcomes of the students.
- ☞ *Collective learning* —the conditions where learning, risk-taking and creativity thrives for the greater good of the school by being co-created and implemented by all stakeholders (including leadership taken by students where the teachers are in the learning position).

This perspective on leadership changes our understanding of "follower" from one that passively receives direction and directives by, to one where the relationships within the school determine that all stakeholders become part of *"doing leadership."*

There is a strong tradition of employing the principles of distributed leadership, albeit not in its purest form, in the education environment, especially about school leadership. However, with the insatiable progress in technology taking on the central role in teaching and learning, and where online and virtual learning-hives will become the norm and school management structures will no longer exist, we are urged to consider alternative leadership models. Also, countries like the United Kingdom are actively exploring the notion of technology-driven learning where non-graduates take on the role of learning facilitators rather than qualified teachers, and we are obliged to ask whether distributed education in its purest form isn't a better model for leadership in the 21st century?

Exit Reflection

Leadership is not accidental, innately endowed, or random. Leadership is a deliberate set of behaviours that are designed to fit the purpose a specific setting. Leadership in the 21st Century is characterised by conflicts between child-centred teaching, learning and assessment and qualitative measurable account-ability; between creating inclusive learning environments and serving the human resource needs of industry; between what is being taught and how much of it should be taught; between integrating technology and developing interpersonal relationships between teacher and learner.

Leadership in education has the moral duty to navigate these conflicting aspects of school life in such a way that young people are morally, spiritually and academically prepared to become active contributing members of democratic societies. In order to achieve this, school leaders have access to a variety of leadership models and styles from which they should choose the most appropriate model and style to empower their teachers to become efficient classroom practitioners.

In this chapter you learned that:

🡒 leadership styles and how your habitual leadership behaviours can either develop or hinder a culture and climate that fosters excellence and mastery;

☞ the importance of purpose as the cornerstone of your leadership behaviours notwithstanding the style or model you choose as you foundation

☞ control and leadership are not synonymous and that in a culture of accountability, you could easily try to take too much control, rather than empower teachers to become intrinsically motivated

VI

MOTIVATION

Sir Richard Branson is known for his adage *if you take care of your staff, your staff will take care of the customers*. The same principle is also true of the teaching profession. If you take care of your teachers and support staff, encourage their emotional well-being, empower them to become experts in their field and foster in them a sense of trust and support, they will do the same in their classrooms. Successful leaders do not only focus sharply on improving their teachers' teaching, learning and assessment (TLA) skills, they also have a direct influence on classroom practice through their efforts to motivate their teachers and create a climate and culture that encourages social, emotional well-being in the work place. Happy teachers make for happy students. Simply put, if you are the motivator in chief, you don't have to become the chief whip. But how do you know how motivated your teachers, and support staff are, and what can you do about improving motivation? Before you jump into the deep end of the motivational pool, we should understand a few necessary, and for the most part, universal principles regarding human motivation.

What Is Motivation?

Motivation is an internal experience that cannot be seen by the people surrounding you. Motivation are the forces within and outside of us that compel us to behave in specific ways in order to meet specific physiological and emotional needs and to achieve specific goals.

Needs are internal motivators. Physiological and psychological needs drive our behaviours in order to sustain life, promote well-being and emotional equilibrium. For instance, if you are thirsty, you are experiencing the physiological need or motivation to drink water. Similarly, if you feel the emotional need that your spouse or best friend should recognise the way you successfully managed to juggle a stressful day at work, a minor family crisis as well as taking the cat to the vet, you have a psychological need for recognition of your ability to calmly multitask.

A modern example of human needs as driver of behaviour, for example, are manifested in the way social media and smart devices have become strong motivational pulling forces. The designers of social media platforms have cleverly exploited this psychological need for acceptance and recognition: the number of *likes* you have received on your LinkedIn post is so significant to you that you are motivated continuously to check who and how many people have *liked* your post.

Goals, on the other hand, are external motivators that

compel us to engage in specific actions. Goals function on multiple levels ranging from wanting to lose weight, to becoming the principal of your school. Even though the prospect of achieving a goal, and the social recognition that goes hand-in-hand with it, are psychological, the stimuli and the actual tangible goal are external in nature.

Together, needs and goals work concomitantly as the drivers of our behaviour. But before we look at the finer details of how we can motivate people to engage in specific behaviours, it is worth taking a look at what behaviour is. Behaviour is the actions a person engages in after experiencing a stimulus (antecedent). Actions inevitably have reactions of consequences based on those reactions. This reaction and its related consequence will determine the continuation of similar behaviour and whether the person experiences the consequence as pleasant or unpleasant, will determine how the person will behave in future. If the consequence was experienced as pleasant, then similar behaviour is certain to reoccur. If the consequence was experienced as unpleasant, then the person will avoid the same behaviour in future. Human behaviour is a complex cycle of antecedents, behaviours and consequences that directs our action as well as the responses of other people in our proximity. For example, as you are sipping your coffee, the *message received* sound on your mobile device pings in your pocket (antecedent). You are internally motivated to check on every instance of feedback received on your latest social media post, and you automatically reach into your pocket to retrieve your phone (behaviour). In doing so, you spill the hot coffee on the table and some of it on your lap (consequence). The hot coffee on your lap is everything but pleasant and you are not pleased with yourself. Minutes later, the ping sounds again, but this time you put the coffee down on the table before you reach for the phone. You have adjusted your behaviour because the consequence of the hot coffee on your lap was decidedly unpleasant. With the new adjusted behaviour of putting the coffee down first, you can enjoy the pleasure of seeing yet another *like* on your social media post.

To take one step a little closer in order to understand what you can do to motivate your teachers and support staff, we need to understand what influences the intensity and quality of motivation. The strength of motivation is how much effort a person will put into a task. The quality of motivation is how compelling the reason and value linked to achieving the goal are. You must understand the intensity and quality of the motivation of your teachers and support staff for you to determine what actions you must take to increase their motivation.

Motivation Theories

Research into applied motivation has proven to have some bad news for those leaders who think that motivation and emotions are not as important as hard figures and facts. If you were planning to introduce a quick and easy, self-sustaining motivation plan, I have bad news for you. The general finding of research into motivation strategies is that *that which is easy is rarely sufficient.* You may ask, then is it worth trying to implement a motivation program at all? The answer is yes, and the place to start is to find a motivation theory that resonates with you, your style of leadership and the vision on which your school has decided.

Expectancy-value Theory

We have now established that there is a need for a motivation program to be designed and implemented. Yet, before you can jump ahead and start motivating our teachers and support staff, it is of some importance to understand why these teachers are not motivated to deliver their best work. The fact is that some people may know exactly why they feel disinterested or bored with a task, they might see why they have a sense of anxiety or fear of another, however, in many situations, it isn't as clear-cut as that. More often than not, we may have a distinct sense of not feeling motivated, yet it feels near impossible for us to put our finger on what causes us to feel such emotions. The most significant of the theories that set out to explain why we feel unmotivated is expectancy-value theory.

Expectancy-value looks at whether an individual expects a particular consequence to occur and what personal value the outcome holds for the individual. In other words, previous experience has taught you that you can expect that the Head of Department for English will cancel a meeting, minutes after you have arrived at the venue. This has become a habit of the HOD and even though it is on the face of it an important meeting to attend, you are not very motivated to be on time to the meeting. The opposite is also true. You have learned from previous experience that the people that arrive first at the local authority meeting gets to choose the freshest sandwiches and you get to have one-on-one time with the keynote speaker. This example has both the expectancy that a specific and pleasant consequence will undoubtedly take place (sandwiches) and it has personal value because you get to discuss your particular situation with a specialist in the field.

By way of summary, expectancy-value theory predicts that if your teachers have an expectation of being able to fulfil a task, and if they can predict a positive outcome of the task, and if those teachers have attached a high personal value to the outcomes of the task, they will be motivated to work hard to reach the expected outcomes.

Social Motivation Theory

There are four factors that we should look at to understand a person's motivation. The first is the *reinforcement value*, in other words, how important is the reward/ reinforcement attached to the behaviour. Will you in fact receive what you expected to receive as a result of the specific action or behaviours? And, if you did get what you expected to get, is that outcome important enough to you? The second is your *subjective estimates*: your assessment of the probability of you being able to achieve the specific result. If you believe you have the ability, skills and knowledge to complete a particular task, you will be more motivated to engage in that task than if you sincerely think you cannot do so.

Situational factors include your expectations about a particular situation based on similar experiences in the past. Remember the example I used above; if you have experienced that the HOD of English usually postpones the department meetings, it will not take many instances of finding closed doors, before you come to expect that these specific meetings (specific situations) will not take place as advertised. Finally, there is a *generalised expectation* that you hold about how life works in your particular part of the world.

One aspect of generalised expectation includes your explanatory style, in other words, whether you look at things through an optimistic or pessimistic lens. Do you look at general events that are non-specific in terms of optimistic opportunities or do you consider general events in terms of specific problems that could hamper your progress?

Consider the following example: imagine, you have a teacher that has just joined your school after about a decade in a small rural school. He has all the right credentials on paper, his interview was spot on, and his TLA strategies are adequate. Yet, when you asked him to join the team of teachers that are exploring the possibility of including more mobile technology in classes, you realise that he is decidedly against the initiative. His body language is passive-aggressive and he does not show much enthusiasm when you approache him about joining the team. If you could imagine yourself into his position, you may gain an understanding of how his expectancy-value contributes to his level of motivation. You could imagine that there is no reward/reinforcement value because the additional responsibility does not come with extra remuneration and he wants to spend time getting his classroom practice right. You could also suppose that a previous experience in dealing with social media (subjective estimation) has proven to him that he is not entirely comfortable with using emerging technology as a learning tool (at his previous school he was more accustomed to using printed media than mobile devices).

The *situational factors* may mean that, despite his optimistic explanatory style and his general positive approach, he doesn't yet feel comfortable in the new environment to admit his inexperience in technology-based teaching and learning, nor to contribute freely to new initiatives. Even, if these are not the exact reasons your new teacher seems less than enthusiastic to add to the new plan of action, the point is that you can do something to motivate him, rather than immediately suspect that he is a bad apple.

Extrinsic and Intrinsic Motivation

Rewards and punishers are external motivators. They have an impact on your behaviour as a result of environmental incentives and consequences such as food, money, praise, attention, tokens, gold stars, scholarships, trophies, certificates, public recognition, a smile and the list goes on. Extrinsic motivation is the result of an unwritten contract that *if you do THIS, then I will give you THAT.* The *this* in the tacit agreement refers to the desired behaviour, and then *that* is the meaningful incentive or reward you would receive in exchange for that response. In essence, it is an old-fashioned bartering system.

We base our understanding of the environmental regulation of motivation on operant conditioning. You *operate* in a specific environment because you have learned through the consequences of your behaviours, how to function in that context. For example, you have determined that greeting the security guard on your way into the parking lot is met with a warm smile. However, if you neglect to say good morning, you receive an unsatisfied disapproving look. The consequence of the smile makes you feel good, it is a pleasant experience and this releases a dose of dopamine in your frontal cortex which is why you feel good. Whereas the consequence of a disapproving look leaves you with a feeling of discomfort, a sense of unpleasantness. Next time you see the guard, your behaviour has been conditioned to say good morning, and thus you have learned to operate efficiently within the environment. Simply put, the smile is a reward, and the disapproving look is a punishment. The use of rewards and punishers as motivators work in exactly the same way.

Incentives and Rewards

An incentive is an event or consequence that attracts or repels a person from engaging in a specific course of action. You expect an incentive as the result of a desired action or response. In other words, for you to behave in the desired way, you must expect that a specific reward or incentive will be the result of that specific behaviour. We learn the value incentives hold through our previous experiences. For instance, the pleasant smell of coffee as you walking into your favourite coffee shop, or the smell of warm waffles as you walk past the confectionary is the rewards for getting up early on a Sunday morning and going to town. You expect the smell will be there and because it is a pleasant experience you like having, you are incentivised to take the specific action that will ensure the pleasant experience. The opposite is also true. The unpleasant smell of decay ensures that you check if you placed the milk in the fridge and if you have closed the fridge door. If you haven't placed the milk in the fridge, you receive the negative incentive of the unpleasant tinge of nausea resulting from the smell in the kitchen when you arrive home. If this happens often enough, you will in future remember to close the fridge door.

Pleasant rewards/incentives don't necessarily result in positive behaviour, and a negative reward doesn't result in negative action. It is important to remember it is possible for you to reward somebody for engaging in undesired behaviours as well.

For example, a mother can reward her two-and-a-half-year-old for his glass-shattering *tantrum-mania* by giving him attention and a sweet to keep him calm while she is doing the weekly grocery run. The next time she enters the grocery store, little Bobby will recognise the setting and remember that there is a reward attached to his theatrics, and what follows is a reward winning (literally) performance.

There is not much difference between little Bobby and your teaching and support staff. I'm not suggesting that your team throw tantrums. However, I must admit that I have experienced, and at times performed, similar theatrics before. In the absence of your leadership in motivation, they will innately resort to behaviours that are incentivised as part of the social interactions that take place, and if you do not set the tone and create the culture in which desired behaviours are rewarded, then there is a significant chance that undesired behaviours will be strengthened through reinforcers such as negative attention.

Day-To-Day Reinforcement of Desired Behaviour

Daily motivation cannot depend on substantial rewards or incentives being handed out. As a matter of fact, over-rewarding will have the opposite effect. For ongoing reinforcement of desired behaviour, as well as for developing a culture of recognising positive, constructive actions, there is nothing as powerful as reinforcing through praise, recognition and affirmation. To make a clear distinction between rewards and incentives on a larger scale and the day-to-day culture of appreciation, we use the term *reinforcement*. However, the principles remain the same.

For continuous reinforcement of the desired behaviour to be effective, you should keep four aspects of giving rewards in mind: immediacy, certainty, personal preference and frequency. Immediacy, as the word suggests, indicates that the time between observing the desired behaviour and giving the reinforcement that strengthens that response or actions, should not be too long. In colloquial terms, once a staff member has been *caught doing the right thing* the reinforcement (compliment, attention, affirmation) should be given at once. For example, a short feedback discussion regarding the actions of the teacher or staff can serve as reinforcement of the desired behaviour and should be specific, pleasant, affirmative and personal. During the discussion, you are recognising the teacher's individual actions, affirming the value of the contribution and showing that the behaviour underwrites the collective vision of the school. It is important to remember that this serves as a reinforcement of desired behaviour and should not be seen as an opportunity for an *even better if you did this* type of discussion.

Secondly, *certainty* points towards the expectancy-value of the individual. The teacher knows that if you see her/him behave in a specific way that s/he will receive some kind of recognition or affirmation. The importance of certainty lies in your own consistency of behaviour. If for instance teachers and support staff cannot predict how you will react to their TLA behaviours, they will be reluctant to show initiative or introduce innovative TLA opportunities. However, if your reaction to the teacher being *caught doing the right thing*, is consistent and the teacher can be certain that a verbal reward will follow, they will be willing to be more creative and take appropriate TLA risks.

Thirdly, the given reinforcement should always be *personal and pleasant*. Research shows that second to money, recognition of individuality is the most potent reinforcer of specific behaviours, and operant conditioning has proven that pleasant consequences will lead to the repetition of behaviours. In other words, if the reinforcement you give the teacher is specific to that teacher and the teacher enjoys receiving the reward or support, then the teacher will engage in the desired behaviour again. As an example, if you know the teacher's name, and some personal details like the names and ages of his children, which school the children are going to etc., you may use this as part of your quick feedback discussion once the teacher was *caught doing the right thing*. The discussion may go like this: *Mr Mtembu, I liked how you explained to the student that his behaviour could make other students feel excluded, and I liked how you made him feel part of the school community. Your tone of voice was strict, yet calm and friendly. Tell me, how is Thabo doing at the new school? Is he settling in well?* The personal nature of the discussion, alongside the specific feedback about what the teacher did well, makes the recognition (reinforcer) pleasant to receive. However, there is a warning in this. Be careful of not sounding condescending and make sure that Mr Mtembu actually has a son called Thabo. There is nothing so discouraging as false praise and the knowledge that your leaders have no idea who you are.

Finally, you should consider the frequency with which you use a specific reinforcement strategy. Using the same strategy all the time and irrespective of the value individuals attach to it, will lead to staff not experiencing the value of being recognised by the principal. I am not suggesting that you stop the *certainty* of receiving a reinforcer, but rather what the actual reinforcer must not become monotonous. For instance, on the one day, you may wish to have a short discussion with the teacher, and on another you may be pressed for time, but have time a bit later in the day to send a quick e-mail, or mention something during the staff briefing. Again, discretion is advised. Even though the mantra is *praise in public*, it can too often seem that you don't treat all teachers and staff equally, and even if nothing can be further from the truth, perceptions can damage your strategy of reinforcing the desired behaviour through praise, recognition and affirmation. The fact is that some teachers just don't get *caught doing the right thing* as often as others. That doesn't mean that they don't actually engage in desired behaviour. It just means that their TLA behaviour is less overt than others. It is your duty to find out what those more introverted teachers are doing well and make an effort to *catch them doing the right thing*. There are many examples where this is possible. You may find that the quieter teacher is not seen outside on the playground, informally building relationships with the learners, because she is busy spending specific time giving and following up on detailed feedback. You don't have to wait for the formal inspection period to see what her assessment feedback looks like: you are the leader and it is your job to find good things to say about everybody. As before, be careful that during your attempt to catch a teacher *doing the right thing*, you don't get distracted and start emphasising the things they have done wrong. You will find mistakes in the day-to-day practice of everybody – including your own. That being said, when you see safeguarding concerns, this will need to be addressed as a matter of urgency, and the reinforcement can wait for later.

Incentive Programs and Reward Events

We hold awards evenings for movie stars, musicians and learners, yet teachers remain in the wings. A significant motivator can be found in incentive programs and award evenings. Incentive programs can take on many forms. Some of the most valuable incentive programs include study bursaries, leadership exchange programs, and attendance at subject-specific international conferences. Insofar as these programs do have a monetary value, however it is important to remember that the most significant benefit for the teacher and support staff usually lies in the awarded self-development opportunities that go hand-in-hand with such incentives. It is essential that teachers and staff on all levels have the opportunity to receive similar incentives and that the criteria for being awarded an incentive is clear and well published by the team. The way in which the outcomes of the reward can be employed to further the school's vision should be an additional criterion to the award criteria, such as the *significant continuous progress* of *all students* or *considerable support to SEND* etc.

Annual awards ceremonies have been a part of school since the invention of soggy sandwiches. In many schools, leadership teams have decided to include a similar program for teachers and support staff, and as with the student version, clear award criteria and expectancy-value is cardinal to the success of the awards ceremony. Another critical aspect of making award ceremonies successful is the fully inclusive nature of the event. You must invite everybody, and everybody must stand a chance of receiving an award. It is also essential that receiving an award as part of such an incentive scheme must not be connected to annual remuneration.

Success criteria for awards ceremonies may include:

- everybody must stand a chance, but not everybody must win;
- rewards/incentives must have personal value for the winner;
- hold open consultation on the criteria for awards and how teacher can qualify for awards;

↬ you must make the criteria for the reward categories public before you start conducting reviews and setting performance targets;

↬ the criteria according to which a winner was chosen must be made public;

↬ Staff may opt out of the reward scheme, but there must not be an expectation that staff must apply for a reward.

↬ introverts must also stand a chance to be awarded;

↬ diversity must be celebrated;

↬ all levels of the school community must be included in the various reward categories;

↬ criteria must not be based on, or include any instance where the abilities or socio-economic status of students can play a role in advancing any specific teacher to win a reward (those teaching disadvantaged and SEND must also be eligible);

↬ where two or more individuals qualify for the same award, do under no circumstance draw a lot to determine the winner;

↬ all those that qualify, must receive the reward, otherwise the cardinal principle of *certainty* is violated, rendering the motivation power of the reward null and void.

Other reward arrangements may include teacher or support staff of the month; 100% attendance for the term; exceptional service to the department and extraordinary service to the school. Whereas the attendance award is objective, it is essential that subjective assessment of service awards or *teacher of the month* awards should be transparent. Please note these are only suggestions, and many leaders may choose to approach incentives in a more authentic way.

The History of Reinforcement

Motivation is a deceivingly complex topic, filled with contradictions and discordances. For example, we have seen that if one of your teachers expects a reward and that teacher is sure that she can achieve the targets, then she will be motivated to behave in the desired way. However, if the used reinforcer is predictable, then motivation will decrease. In other words, when the teacher is *caught doing the right thing* and she can predict that your response (reinforcer) is going to be, *that's what we want to see Ms Turner,* your well-intended reinforcer will become a cliché and lose its power as reinforcement.

An added contradiction that is typical of motivation is that money, as a rule, is a stronger reinforcer than praise, except if the remuneration package of the teacher allows for all her basic needs to be met with enough left for savings and some luxuries, then praise is a stronger reinforcer. We've seen that a reinforcer must be immediate for it to be effective, however all reinforcement can be given immediately. In such situations, is the expectancy of achieving the goal, and not the actual goal, that keeps motivation levels high. For example, your teacher has been working towards achieving his performance targets. He knows that if he reaches his value-added targets, the incentive he will receive is to attend an international conference on innovative TLA practice. While he has his eye on the ball, so to speak, his motivation levels are high, even though the reinforcement is not given immediately, the expectation of being able to attend the conference keeps him motivated. After he has achieved the targets and participated in the conference, his motivation levels will decrease until he has set new goals and attached them to another incentive that has personal value for him. Thus, it is the expectation that engenders the motivation and not the actual incentive/reward.

The history of previous reinforcement is also one of the contradictions in motivation. Research has proven that there are three aspects of the history of reinforcement that has an impact on motivation levels. An experiment with rats, as always, showed some surprising findings. The trial was to give a colony of rats a high reward (257 pellets of food) on completion of a maze-based task. At the onset of the experiment, the rats learned very quickly how to reach the end the maze and their completion time improved dramatically after each turn. The second colony received a fair reward (16 pellets of food) and as can be expected their performance was mediocre as was their reward, but they too showed progress in completing the maze. At a specific point, the researchers decided to reduce the high reward to the same level as the second group, and the results were dramatic. The first group's performance tumbled to low levels despite the fact that they, by now, knew the maze pretty well. The second set of rats, however, maintained a consistently mediocre performance.

What was clear from the experiment was that if the reward at the onset is high, with no scope for receiving some larger rewards, motivation to perform well falls through the floor. And, if mediocrity is all you desire, then a predictable, low-level reward is given regardless whether the subject, the rat in this case, performs better or worse over the course of time. However, the most surprising aspect was yet to come. The researchers decided to introduce a third group to the experiment. This group started their maze activity receive a meagre reward per completion (1 pellet of food), and with every successful completion of the task, the researchers incrementally enlarged the rewards. What they found was that these rats continued to improve, and very soon outperformed the first group's achievements in a much faster time.

The moral of the story, not that we want to compare anybody to rats, is to start rewarding your teachers and support staff with smaller rewards at the beginning of the motivation program and then to incrementally, over the year, increase the value of the rewards — will sustain motivation. Giving incentives, rewards or reinforcers (all these terms used synonymously in this case), in practice, means that personal gain is forthcoming and that the situation that the teacher or support staff is currently involved in, has taken an unpredicted turn for the better. Therefore, rewards work. They increase the desired behaviour, however as they become routinely predictable, they lose their capacity to trigger the dopamine release that drives behaviour, and the teacher wants more of a reward to continue with the desired behaviour. In this case desired behaviour will include planning and implementing interesting, engaging and effective TLA opportunities.

Punishers

A punisher is a stimulus in the environment that, when experienced, decreases specific related behaviours. In other words, during a whole staff meeting, a young and energetic SEND support teacher keeps on talking while the announcements for the week are being made. This is not the type of behaviour you expect from your teachers and support staff. As a result, you stop talking, and a quick, disapproving glance at the support teacher serves as a punisher. He realises his erroneous ways, and stops talking. The unpleasant consequence of talking during announcements the *look* and therefore, the undesired behaviour is discontinued. In the same way as reinforcers, punishers don't discriminate between good or bad behaviour, it just encourages the discontinuation of conduct. For example, if you *have caught a teacher doing the right thing*, and after a short pleasant reinforcer, you decide to reprimand her for all the wrong things she has done that you want to talk about to her. This is seen as a punishment. In future, the teacher will not be engaging in the desired behaviour for fear of being *caught doing the right thing* and then getting into trouble for all the other possible problems there might be.

The Problem with Punishment

Punishers are omnipresent. As a matter of fact, because of the relative ease with which you can punish a person, and the corresponding immediacy of the impact of punishment, it is a popular method of motivating people to stop undesired behaviours. Less emotional energy, forethought and effort goes into punishing a person. It is quite useful in the short term and needs much less creativity to inflict. However, the side effects of punishment are problematic. The emotional fallout of punishment is almost allways negative and results in ineffective relationships between the punisher and the punished. Distrust, aversion and a general disinclination towards the vision espoused by the punisher are some of the lesser challenging affects.

Sustained punishment can result in learned helplessness, where the teacher or support staff disengages entirely and become utterly dependent on external stimuli to function. It can also lead to depression, stress-related physiological impairments and irregular school attendance. Besides, by making punishment your go-to strategy to direct the behaviours of the teachers and support staff, means that you are also modelling an ineffective method of how to deal with stressful situations. Inevitably this trickles down, and in the end, punishment will become the teachers' preferred method of behaviour management, leaving students feeling helpless and unhappy. Students that suffer from helplessness and that feel depressed do not make sustained, efficient progress. Therefore, one lazy strategy can sink your entire vision if not used sparingly and judiciously.

When is Punishment the Right Thing?

As previously implied, you should not entirely abandon punishers. There are situations where punishment is needed. Neglecting to safeguard students would be an example where punishment should be considered immediately. Actions that warrant penalty is when teachers relinquish their TLA duties, in cases of non-attendance as well as poor punctuality. When using punishers as a way to deter inappropriate behaviour, the specific actions and related punishment should be a matter of policy and must be included in the teacher handbook. As in the case of an incremental approach to rewards, punishers should also be progressive in their gravity. Labour law and union guidelines are often the best places to find guidance as to how and when to use punishers. I also suggest you involve all union representatives in setting up the attendance and performance management policies. This consultation should receive priority and union input on the specific punishments that may be used if the policies are breached, should explicitly indicate that the union suggested and agreed on such consequences.

It is vital that rigorous record keeping on your side goes hand-in-hand with using a punisher as deterrent for inappropriate behaviour. Verbal reprimands, letters of warning, a formal *notice to improve* suspension and termination should at all times go hand-in-hand with specific undesirable actions, with the relevant dated and notes recorded and available for the staff member to see. Needless to say, the information and details regarding punishers are confidential and should be treated as such. The specific staff member's rights under the law should at all times be respected and adhered to.

The mantra of *praise in public and punish in private* comes to the forefront again. Naming and shaming is not only the best way to create a toxic work environment, but it is also teeters on the verge of being illegal.

How should I deal with Suspending a Teacher?

Unfortunately, there are cases in which you would not follow the process of verbal and written warnings, and it is necessary to suspend the staff member immediately. In any case where the staff member poses a physical threat to students, colleagues, parents or visitors to the school, that member of staff should immediately be suspended and removed from the campus.

Policies regarding suspension should be clear and you should have a document that lays out the staff member's rights and next steps during this time. This must include contact details of support agencies that s/he may use for legal and emotional support, as well as prohibited behaviours during the time of suspension. What next actions s/he can expect from the school and the timeframe within which these steps will take place. The suspension is not a formal hearing and formal disciplinary procedures will have to follow.

Formal disciplinary documents should always be ready insofar as unfortunate events that may lead up to suspension are usually unexpected. Confidentiality remains of the utmost importance, and it is inappropriate to *make an example* of the situation or person to deter others from unwanted behaviours. Keep in mind that, if you over (or under) react, your actions will be included in the ensuing investigations and therefore, suspending a staff member should be fair and warranted.

In addition to the suspension and related documentation that is provided to the staff member that is under investigation, you should have a personal, face-to-face conversation with the aggrieved party (student, colleague or parent) and inform them of the suspension. It is vital that you press on them the significance of confidentiality and that any possible intimation of gossiping or witch hunting will have deleterious results. This conversation should go hand-in-hand with a document that reiterates the content of the communication, the rights of the aggrieved party as well as the rights of the accused teacher or staff member. Clear records and acknowledgement of receiving these documents must be signed and dated and kept safe. In addition, all subsequent communication with all parties should be dated and followed up in writing (from both the aggrieved and accused sides), with the explicit understanding that these documents will be used in formal proceedings.

Intrinsic Motivation

The gold standard of motivation is intrinsic motivation. Intrinsic motivation is your natural proclivity towards exploring the world around you as well as your own abilities and interests. It is the drive you experience that makes you want to master your environment. It is also the instinctive striving for personal growth and psychological need satisfaction. Intrinsically motivated people actively look for novelty, optimal challenges, and they work hard to extend their talents and capabilities; through exploration and learning. In other words, they develop, and they grow. The characteristics of intrinsically motivated teachers and support staff are that they show initiative, they act spontaneously, strive to learn and increase their ability in the classroom as well as in leadership, they show higher task persistence (they just don't give up) and they experience positive emotions and well-being. The key to understanding intrinsic motivation is that you don't have to reward people for behaving in the desired way, the behaviour itself, the very act of being busy with something interesting, is enough of a reward for them. It must be said, that even the most dedicated and intrinsically motivated people must still eat, and you can't suddenly decide to stop paying your best performing teachers, just because they are driven from within.

If we consider the outcomes achieved after you used extrinsic motivation strategies, and compare them with the results you achieved based on intrinsic motivation, we notice that intrinsically motivated individuals are healthier, happier and more self-assured than those driven by rewards. You will be forgiven to think that all you should do is find a way to turn your reward seeking teachers into intrinsically motivated teachers. It is not that easy. Intrinsic motivation is highly dependent on the interests and self-development of the individual and is only useful if your teachers don't have to engage in monotonous or uninteresting tasks, such as grading uninspiring exams or completing a range of administrative duties that are necessary, but are as dull as dust. In such cases, extrinsic motivation (in the form of avoiding punishment for work not completed on time) is the type of motivation that keeps the wheels turning.

Which Strategy Works Best?

There are a few facts to keep in mind when you consider tangible rewards are as motivation. The first is that if an intrinsically motivated person is unexpectedly given a physical award for work done based on their interest and curiosity, the intrinsic motivation wanes in efficacy. The second is that expected physical rewards interfere with the process and quality of TLA insofar as the award shifts the teacher's attention away from achieving mastery over their environment or domain in order to achieving the tangible reward. Once the teacher has received the prize, he typically quits the desired behaviours and returns to ineffective run-of-the-mill TLA behaviour. Thus, physical rewards put the teachers and support staff at risk of becoming passive processors of information and robotic instructors rather than creative problem solvers. A final point is that tangible rewards inhibit the development of independent self-regulation.

Moving From External to Internal Regulation to Self-determination

External regulation, or the dependence on rewards to motivate teachers to behave in specific ways, is not always negative. In leading change initiatives, the use of external motivation to introduce the new TLA behaviour can be used to significant effect. One way that rewards are useful is if they are unexpected and verbal. A second way to use rewards is to only give rewards for tasks that have low interest but high social importance. Besides, it is possible to facilitate the development of intrinsic motivation through a well-designed and explicit plan. Facilitating the development from external to intrinsic motivation should be included in the leading change plan from the start by incorporating the following four steps: external regulation, introjected regulation, identified regulation and integrated regulation. It is vital that you are transparent about the process of internalisation from the start. You should tell staff from the onset of the program that you aim to foster intrinsic motivation and which steps they should expect to see. Research has indicated that when people have knowledge and understanding of the procedures that they are about to embark on, they move much faster from one step the next step and this allows for achieving integrated regulation much faster.

Step 1: Establish Self-regulation

In the first place, you can achieve external regulation of behaviour by providing external rewards (and if needed punishers). As stated earlier, verbal and unexpected reinforcement works best and may keep your teachers engaging in the new TLA behaviour. You may aim to be on the lookout to *catch your teacher doing the right thing* or you may want to do *drop-in* class visitations: naturally teachers must be aware that these can happen from time to time and that they will not be used to evaluate their performance.

Step 2: Establish Internalised Mastery

As your teachers become more confident with the new TLA behaviour, you should have a discussion with them in which you explain that there is an expectation that they internalise the new methods of teaching, and that the collective aim of the school, and therefore all members of the school community, is to aim for mastery of the new methods. You should explain why putting effort into the new practices are worth the while, how these practices can contribute to improved outcomes for the students and how the *mastery* of these methods will allow the achievement of the new vision.

Teachers and support staff who find the rationale convincing and personally satisfying for why the new behaviour is important, generally put forward a much more significant effort in engaging in the desired new practices. Thus, through this discussion you are aiming to create awareness of the process of internalisation and to initiate introjected regulation. You are setting the stage for teachers to take self-control over the new TLA behaviours by internalising the rewards and punishers. The only way to facilitate them to do this is to continuously provide the opportunity for self-evaluation and planned adjustment of behaviours. This adaptation of action is an internal process that you have little influence over except for giving time and chance for the teacher to *reflect, review and adjust*. One way of facilitating the process of reflecting, reviewing and adjusting is to introduce a peer-to-peer mentoring system (of which a little bit more later).

Step 3: Establish Identified Self-regulation

The third step towards intrinsic regulation is identified regulation where you start to attach personal importance to the now established TLA behaviour. This is where a sense of achieving mastery comes into fruition and your role as leader, is to vocalise the importance and prospect of emerging *mastery*. For you to move teachers and support staff towards identified regulation, you should use the term mastery in all your communication and discussions.

You should ask what does it look like to have achieved mastery in teaching and learning? You should focus on continuous professional development (CPD) - how to master TLA behaviours. You should allocate time for the sharing of mastery of practice into the academic week. It is possible to move teachers and support staff towards identified regulation. Again, using the peer-to-peer mentoring system as the catalyst for working towards identified regulation, may be the most efficient way to keep teachers focussed on their *emerging mastery*.

Step 4: Establish Mastery as Benchmark

Finally, integrated regulation is the now internal process of self-awareness and synthesis with Self. This is when you can say *this is who I am, I am a master teacher*. There is a difference between integrated regulation and intrinsic locus of control. Where intrinsic locus of control is based on interests, enjoyment and inherent satisfaction, integrated regulation may include internally driven behaviours that a teacher may not find interesting, and even experience as tiresome. Nevertheless, because these behaviours form an integral part of the mastery of their teaching and learning, teachers are internally driven to participate in such behaviours. For example, data analysis is not every teacher's cup of tea, yet when conducted in an informative way, it empowers the teacher to know and understand their students' learning needs. Despite the tedious nature of data analysis, since it contributes to the *mastery* of teaching and learning, the internally driven teacher will complete the data analyses to an excellent standard to improve their TLA behaviours.

Exit Reflection

There is no such thing as a quick fix motivation strategy. Motivation is not quick, it is not easy and it is everything but simple. Human behaviour is inextricably linked with emotions, and our emotions are the drivers of our behaviours. Therefore, getting a solid understanding of what motivates people and the value they assign to rewards and incentives is crucial.

Motivating your teachers, support staff and by extension your students is a deliberate set of behaviours, strategies and actions that you must keep a constant eye on. Motivating your teachers is not a duty that can be delegated into a dusty corner of your to do list, and it is most certainly not a task that can be relegated as a peace-sake measure to keep some young and impatient future leader occupied. Motivating your teachers is your job. One that must be integrated into every aspect of your journey to mastery and self-determination.

As leader you should ask yourself:

- ☞ What motivates me to become a masterful leader?
- ☞ What type of incentives is valuable to me? Am I generally an internally (intrinsic) or externally (extrinsic) motivated?
- ☞ What are the unmet needs of students and staff? How do these unmet needs influence their behaviour?
- ☞ What are the unmet goals of students and staff? How do these unmet needs influence their behaviour?

VII

THE SELF-DETERMINED LEADER

It is in our nature to be busy with exploring or manipulating our environment; as humans, we are inherently active. When this activity taps into and includes our psychological needs, we feel interested and enjoyment. Three psychological needs are instinctive in humans: autonomy, competence and relatedness. And when we fulfil these three psychological needs, we feel a sense of control over our destiny; a feeling that we are interested and enjoying the things we are busy with for our satisfaction.

Autonomy

When we choose what we want to do and how we want to do it, we yearn for decision-making flexibility. We want our ideas to be our own, and we want to be the ones that determine our actions - instead of allowing somebody tell us what to do. We want our behaviours to originate from our interests, preferences, wants and desires. **Autonomy** is the psychological need to experience a sense of self-direction and personal validation. If you have decided to cultivate self-determination as the main mo-tivation strategy in your leadership tool-kit, autonomy is the first step towards fostering self-determination.

For teachers to demonstrate their level of autonomy they should be able to show the following five items:

- ⚹ their decisions represent their most important values and feelings;
- ⚹ they strongly identify with the things they do;
- ⚹ their actions are in line with who they are;
- ⚹ their whole-self supports the decisions they make;
- ⚹ their choices are steadily informed by the things about which they care.

When the environment and the interpersonal relationships a teacher may experience on a day-to-day level counteracts these five items, the teacher's autonomy is removed from, and s/he find her/him-self in a situation where they are being controlled.

For you to create a climate that becomes autonomy supportive, you need to foster the trust and empowerment that encourages decision autonomy and the alignment of the teacher's beliefs and ethos with their TLA behaviours. These enabling conditions include:

- ☞ taking your teacher's perspectives and adopting their frames of reference (put yourself in their shoes);
- ☞ to be welcoming and inviting to the thoughts, feelings, ideas of your teachers during discussions about what the most effective TLA behaviours are;
- ☞ to support your teachers' capacity for autonomous self-regulation through continuous training and self-development opportunities.

As example, you can provide a teacher with the opportunity to be seconded to the leadership team for a term, or shadow (follow) a leader for several weeks to see how and why that leader makes decisions. This strategy will improve their understanding of the role and responsibilities of the leaders and allows the teacher to reflect on how s/he would behave in a similar situation.

If you want to create the right conditions for *autonomy*, you must actively and deliberately develop opportunities where your teachers can work in a self-directed way. This is not always very easy, because the very nature of schools insist that timetables and schedules are precise and flawless. However, in practical terms, when your teachers are planning lessons, creating assessments and finding the most optimal TLA practices to promote continuous progress, you must trust that they are the specialists in their field. You must accept that self-direction in their classroom is probably the most efficient way of providing the opportunity for self-direction. Another example could be the way your teachers give progress feedback to their students. A teacher may want to use a variety of methods to efficiently provide feedback to students, whether verbal or written, self or peer feedback. You should support the autonomy of the teacher to provide feedback that is specific, relevant, positive and constructive. The leadership behaviour that you should engage in to support autonomy includes:

- listening to, accepting and allowing teachers and support staff to work in their way;
- nurturing the teacher or support staff's inner motivational resources, in other words allowing them to work in such a way as to find flow;
- relying on and trusting in informational language rather than mountains of administration and record keeping that is supposed to prove accountability;
- acknowledging and accepting expressions of negative emotions – feeling worried or dissatisfied is not a sign of treachery, but rather a sign that they actually care;
- allowing teachers and support staff to feel comfortable with failing and learning, rather than to fail and be punished.

To develop your teachers' and support staff's competence you should provide the opportunity for each individual to work at optimal challenge in an aspect of their development that interests them. You should provide specific, applicable, relevant, positive and constructive progress feedback and, like in autonomy, provide a feeling of being safe to fail.

Practice What You Preach

Your behaviours as a leader either become autonomous behaviours supportive or lead to a controlling environment. To establish mastery driven self-determination among teachers you should adopt behaviours that:

✎ nurture the inner motivational resources of the teachers (in other words allowing teachers to move from external regulation to internal regulation);

✎ provide explanations and rationales for why and how you make decisions;

✎ promote listening emphatically and use non-controlling language in response;

✎ be patient and allow time for self-paced learning and adjusting;

✎ acknowledge and accept your teachers' expressions and negative emotions.

Competence

It is also instinctive to human nature to seek **competence** in controlling our behaviour and environment. We want to be good at what we do, and it is in our nature to want to be seen to be *the best*. When your teachers have the opportunity to engage in activities that offer levels of complexity and difficulty that is precisely right for their current skills and knowledge, then the psychological fulfilment of competence is at its highest. Your teachers' need for competence generates the willingness to look for optimal challenges; drives them to take on these challenges; and allows them to exert the effort and strategic thinking that empowers them to master the problem.

When we are busy with mastering challenges, we find enjoyment in the behaviour and actions that lead to mastery. We experience this pleasure in three ways: the first is *peak experiences*, where we are primarily spectators to events in the environment but derive such joy from these experiences that they leave a substantial impact on us. An example may be the sports coach that watches her team execute every strategy to the point of near perfection. She is not actively engaged on the court, but from the expression on her face, you can see she is wholly involved and in the grips of peak experience.

The second way of experience enjoyment of a challenge is called *peak performance*. Peak performance is when we are in our element, actively working, in collaboration with others, to achieve a goal that we find exciting; where the challenge, complexity and level of difficulty is just right. However, the opposite is also true. If the level of complexity of a task or TLA behaviour is too low or beyond the teacher's current capabilities, there will not be a need for competence, but rather the emotions of boredom or helplessness will become the predominant sentiment. If you have ever seen a curriculum team work on the preparation of the TLA plan for the next academic year, and you see that their interactions become like a dance - specific rhythms that drive the initiatives, planned assessments and innovate strategies forward take place in perfect concert – then you have witnessed peak performance.

The final way, which forms the essence of enjoyment, is a psychological state called *flow*. Flow occurs when we are engaged in an activity or behaviour that involves such a deep level of engagement that self-awareness and the awareness of place and time become absorbed by the action. Flow is such a pleasurable experience that we often engage in the same activity over and over again to be able to experience the flow again. Teachers often describe teaching specific lessons as *having the time of their lives*, or that he feels like he *was in "that teaching zone"*. These are all synonymous with the state of flow, which in turn is the most potent motivating force we have.

The structure within which competence can be developed will include:

↦ communicating clear expectation of what the outcomes must look like and specific procedures that are non-negotiable such as safeguarding of students, attendance and punctuality and recordkeeping of student achievement;

↦ providing the opportunity for teachers and support staff to find optimal challenge;

↦ providing encouragement, and every so often a shoulder to cry on;

↦ providing individualised continuous professional development according to the individual's performance management plan;

↦ providing performance feedback that is timely and constructive.

Become a Catalyst for Competence and Mastery

As leader, you should direct your leadership behaviours in such a way that all the stakeholders in the school are acutely aware of the high expectations you hold of them. It is your challenge to find opportunities within the teacher's scope and duties that can become the catalyst for the need to develop competence. You may think to yourself that there is no way that you can know what each teacher's level of skills and knowledge development is, or whether they will find a task intrinsically interesting or not. The fact is that you don't have to. During the implementation of a positive performance management plan, you have the opportunity to empower each teacher and support staff member to direct their own path towards competence, and in effect your duty is to create the climate of trust that allows each individual to set their own targets in order to achieve competence. Your knowledge of how to set the scene for peak experience, peak performance and flow to take place, becomes the strongest tool in your arsenal of motivating your teachers and support staff.

Relatedness

In the same way as the need for autonomy and competence are instinctive to human behaviour, **relatedness,** the need to belong, is one of the most influential antecedents to behaviour. *Relatedness* is the psychological need to establish and maintain warm emotional bonds and attachment with others. We all experience joy through the closeness when we are interacting with caring and responsive friends - this includes the family members you could consider as personal friends as well as being part of the same clan. Hand-in-hand with relatedness goes *recognition*, both regarding appreciating our individuality and independence, as well as recognising and celebrating our achievements and competence. And, at the heart of *receiving recognition* lies a deep seeded *respect* for our *humanness*, the existential *organismic self* that governs every individual. (We are all organisms, and each organism is distinctly unique, the organismic-self is, therefore, those characteristics, abilities, innate capabilities, competencies, talents, imperfections and faults that make each human inimitable. Accordingly, the term *organismic-self* can best be described as the *you-est you, that you can be*.) If you create a culture and climate in which teachers can feel safe to express and grow their organismic-self, you are setting the scene for relatedness to develop.

The primary condition that involves the need for relatedness is social interaction. And, where there is a possibility of warmth, care, mutual recognition, and respect, these social interactions will satisfy the need for relatedness. However, where there is an expectation of controlling relationships, contempt and belittling, then the need for self-protection supersedes warmth and care. The need for relatedness remains. However, it now is based on distrust of the other, which becomes the predominant emotion within that environment. In other words, if you fail to create a climate of respect, recognition and psychological safety, the only relatedness that will form will be the establishing of cliques and *in-groups* whose aim is to protect those within the group and destroy those on the outside.

Relatedness is strongly linked with the types of interpersonal relationships you encourage in your school. Our communal relationships are based on the trust, respect, reciprocity and recognition that fosters well-being. You should not think that all relationships within the school environment are either wholly exchange-based or completely-communal-based.

Exchange-based or transactional relationships link individual teachers through a common purpose and their relationships depend on goodwill and reciprocity. Communal-based inter-personal relationships evokes the feeling of family. Strong bonds develop and a strong sense of selflessness is evident.

Within the various teams, roles and responsibilities, people who share commonalities and interests will form. Friendships will grow and even the odd romantic relationship or marriage may develop. There will also be groups that place a high premium on their privacy, individuality and space. At face value, they may seem to be more exchange-based in the way they approach relationships with colleagues, yet, where the climate is right, they also aspire to realise the shared vision that the whole school aims to achieve. In any staffroom and classroom, there is a golden in-between where exchange and communal relationships coexist for the benefit of the students. And the value that this golden in-between contributes to the progress and well-being of the students is determined by the culture and climate you create.

The benefits of relatedness need satisfaction is more significant than one may think. When the relatedness needs of your teachers and support staff are fulfilled they experience emotional, physical and cognitive well-being that in turn augments engagement, development and effectiveness in the work place. Research has found that *in the school setting the relatedness to one's teachers, relatedness to one's peers and relatedness to one's family and community are robust and reliable predictors of how a student will engage including how much effort he will put forth during school.* And, as I have stated before, if the teachers and support staff are happy, then your students will be happy too. This in turn increases relatedness, which leads to better student progress. In simpler terms, if your teachers and support staff feel emotionally connected to and interpersonally involved with their colleagues, then they believe that their colleagues are genuinely looking out for them. This increases the satisfaction of the relatedness need, which in turn boosts internalization and intrinsic motivation. In other words, we care because we feel cared for. If our related physical, psychological and cognitive well-being, needs are fulfilled, in other words, if we feel cared for, our brains release oxytocin and vasopressin. These are both hormones that regulate social bonding, stress regulation and emotional reactivity. Therefore, teachers and support staff who experience a continual tide of relatedness are consistently happier, more enthusiastic and they feel less depressed or anxious. If we are more able to regulate our stress and control our emotional reactivity, we will develop fewer stress-related illnesses, which in turn means less time off work, resulting in a win-win situation. Putting it all together, when we are engaged in opportunities that allow for self-direction, autonomy support, optimal challenge, positive feedback on progress and cooperative relationships, we will experience enjoyment. You have to create these opportunities and facilitate and support the conditions that can foster enjoyment.

Relatedness is developed by providing time and place for social interaction and communal relationships to grow through collaboration and shared responsibility. Your responsibility to show and facilitate involvement is to model the ideal cooperative relationships. You can do this by:

- taking time to listen and reflect on others' concerns;
- showing care and feeling empathy for others' situations, needs and desires;
- having detailed knowledge of your teachers' and support staff's workload, what happens to them day in and day out as well as appropriate aspects of their personal lives (distance they travel to work, their own children's general progress and well-being, adversity that can impact on work/life);
- expressing appropriate and professional affection, liking and appreciation for the behaviours of the teacher;
- truly enjoying to be with other people;
- sharing personal resources, such as time, attention, energy, interest and emotional support.

Dr Jacques Mostert

Why Must You Apply Motivation Theory to Practice?

A person's motivation cannot be separated from her social context. In the same way, like a child's motivation is affected by her teachers and peers; or how a coach influences an athlete, the culture and climate of her school affects a teacher. The environment can either be nurturing, or it can be frustrating or undermining the teacher's motivation. There are five areas of application that you should consider when you design and implement a motivation plan for your school: education, work, physical health, personal well-being and sense of community.

If you and your teachers have a better knowledge and understanding of the tenets that underpin motivation you will have a stronger ability to develop intrinsic motivation. Moreover, as we will see in the following sections, competency (being educated in a specific subject discipline) contributes to the person's sense of self-determination, which in turn also improves motivation.

The second area of application is that of work. Work plays a significant role in our experience of having personal value, purpose and meaningfulness. Without feeling a sense of purpose and meaningfulness we experience a sense of worthlessness and helplessness which in turn undermines our capacity to be intrinsically motivated. In the same way, a sense of helplessness also contributes to your negative expectancy-value: in other words, if you expect that your work will not be recognised, and the work you are doing holds little if any personal value for you, you will not be motivated, no matter how hard any leader tries. Work gives us meaning and purpose, and if we remove that sense of meaning and purpose, it will be difficult to feel motivated.

Physical health is a significant contributor to motivation. Because we have physiological needs, if those needs are not met, we will instinctively focus on having those physiological needs met rather than engage in complex tasks which may lead us to achieve a goal. Physical health also contributes to cognitive health, and if your mind is bright because you have had enough sleep, healthy nutrition and you are physically active, then you will have the mental power to focus on achieving your goal.

In the same way, the personal well-being of your teachers that results from a sense of autonomy, a sense of having healthy and promoting interpersonal relationships and their ability to develop their capacity regarding professional and private development. Personal well-being negates the impact of the inevitable stressors that are part and parcel of everyday life. Without such personal well-being, these stressors will build up like plaque and can cause an emotional breakdown if not addressed.

Finally, a sense of community at school fosters relatedness and feeling included in the school community. A sense of gratitude for that which you have and how much you are appreciated at school can help you to feel motivated to become the best possible leader you can be. Selfless contributions to community charities, either through time or contributing your expertise on a pro bono level will enable you to form a better understanding of the individuals in your school community and how you can contribute to their personal development.

Engagement is how actively involved your teachers and support staff are in the TLA behaviour in your school. If your teachers and staff feel entirely engaged, you will see that they are on-task, persistent, show more significant effort and emerging *mastery*. They will show emotional engagement through increased interest, enthusiasm and enjoyment of what they are doing. They will demonstrate cognitive engagement through strategic thinking, independent learning and research and innovative problem solving and finally, agentic engagement through constructive, positive contributions and willingness to take risks to improve the effectiveness of teaching and learning. On a practical level, it means that you must create the environmental conditions that involves and satisfies the need for *autonomy*, *competence* and *relatedness*.

Understanding Why

Whether you have been successful at motivating your teachers and support staff, or at the implementation of an initiative to increase staff attendance and punctuality, it is always important to know the answer to the question *why*. On one level, you would look at the strategies you used and evaluate which of the approaches worked well and which of the methods should improve. On a different level, you will always have to consider the *human* aspects of behaviour. For example, *why* did a problem with punctuality and attendance start, *why* did it persist and *why* were you successful or not in improving the timeliness of staff? The answer to *why* you were successful or not is called a causal attribution, and it is vital that you understand your causal attributions and how they influence your behaviour as well as that of others. From the plethora of attribution theories, we will be looking at three ways you could look at the reasons *why* people behave in the ways they do. The first is called *naïve psychology*, the second is *mastery orientation* and in the third place, *explanatory style*.

Naïve psychology looks at the reasons we, as the observers, attribute to an individual's behaviour. Why do people behave the way they do? When bad or good things happen, at some point during the aftermath of an incident, you (we all) have to come to an attribution choice point. In other words, we need to decide *why* something happened, and why a teacher or member of the support staff behaved in a specific way. The reason why can be ascribed to one of two attributions be that the behaviour was either dispositional (because of who the person is) or it can be the specific situation (how the context and environment impacts on the person). The *disposition attribution* means that they, on some level, had the intention to behave in a specific way. Because they intended to engage in particular actions, ór their cognitive ability would not allow them to deal with a situation in a different way ór because their reactions are typical of their personality and explanatory style (as you will see a bit later). The *situational attribution* explains how a specific situation or environment influenced the individual's behaviour. It could be that his skills and competency contributed to the particular action (that's how he was taught to do things, and he knows no other way). Or it could be that the task was too complicated for him or it could be that random, non-related incidents contributed to a series of (un)fortunate events that contributed to the specific event taking place.

For example, consider the reason Mr Peterson is consistently late to your Monday morning meetings. You will have to decide what you are going to do about his punctuality. Because it is setting a wrong example and even though you follow the strategy of praise in public and punish in private, you are worried that the rest of the staff will think it is ok to not attend the first and most important meeting of the week. Also, there have been situations where Mr Peterson has not disseminated necessary information to his students because he was not there for the morning meeting. This is a typical attribution choice point: *why* is he behaving like this?

You could assume that, on the one hand, Mr Peterson's is somewhat stubborn and has a rather relaxed attitude (the dispositional attribution) towards your leadership. He has been a teacher for much longer than you have been alive and he sees these meetings as a waste of time. On the other hand, it could be that specific situation on a Monday doesn't allow him to be on time, no matter how hard he tries. You decide that you would instead find the facts rather than jump to the disposition attribution. This is always the best course of action to follow. You find out that Mr Peterson's granddaughter has been ill with an incurable disease and he and his wife are taking care of her family. On Monday mornings, his wife takes their daughter for dialysis in the adjoining town, and he is responsible for the school run of their seven and five-year-old grandchildren. The *situational attribution* thus doesn't allow him to be on time, and because he is quite an old school type of teacher (*disposition attribution*) and he doesn't feel comfortable making his problems yours. Having the facts and coming to the correct reason *why* means you can make appropriate decisions about his Monday morning punctuality.

This is common knowledge, yet it is surprising how many people come to the wrong conclusion as to why something happened, which in turn spurs them on to respond in a specific way. Our instinctive proclivity to make assumptions is like a default position we return to when it comes to deciding *why* people behave in a particular way.

In practice, keeping naïve psychology at the forefront of your mindfulness will probably be the best approach you can follow in developing your interpersonal relationships with teachers, support staff, parents, members of the community and indeed with yourself.

Explanatory style, in short , is whether you have an optimistic or pessimistic outlook on life. There is enough evidence to suggest that explanatory style is an instinctive aspect of personality that is, albeit only in part, genetic. Both optimism and pessimism are patterns of thought that we use to **explain** to ourselves *why* something happened (or *why* a future event could take place). A pessimistic explanatory style suggests that the reasons for our failures are internal, because of our ability, intelligence, or skills. The person with a pessimistic explanatory style believes that the fault is constant and stable and that these bad things always happen to them only because they are not bright enough, attractive enough or not from an important enough family etc. They believe that the events that lead to failure are uncontrollable and specific to them. Conversely, an optimistic explanatory style attributes reasons for failure to external events are universal. In other words, we all fail at some point, and usually, the negative situation can be because of poor situational circumstances. The circumstances leading to failure are temporary and impersonal, and through personal intervention, she can learn from mistakes to change the outcomes.

For example, Mrs Dlamini prefers to not participate in planning meetings because she believes that her views have no impact or importance. Her grade 5 class has not been able to achieve their progress targets. The students that she was assigned are less capable than those of Mrs Cele's students, and Mrs Dlamini has many more students with SEND. She is always given these students because the head of the foundation phase doesn't like her, over which she has no control. In general, she feels that she has had an evil eye on her since childhood because if something can go wrong, it will go wrong with her. On the other hand, Mrs Cele's class does have fewer SEND students. However, she has many more students that arrive hungry at school. She realised that if she starts the day with a lesson in life skills by asking different students to make some toast for everybody, she can create a climate of cooperation and a feeling of community and family among the students in her class. She realises that poverty influences everybody and because she herself cannot afford to pay for the daily bread, she negotiated with the local grocery store to sponsor day-old bread (that would have been thrown away) for her breakfast club. The difference between a pessimistic and optimistic approach makes a difference in how a teacher will approach the same set of circumstances.

There isn't much you can do to change the explanatory style of your individual teachers. You can create a culture in which you encourage teachers and support staff to use their explanatory styles to the benefit of the school. For example, when it comes to problems that need outside of the box creative solutions, you will ask Mrs Cele to help you find a way. When it comes to looking at the practicality of new procedures, setting up processes for health and safety as well as doing risk assessments for trips or other initiatives, your best bet would be to include Mrs Dlamini on your panel. Her instinctive propensity to find the risk in situations will come in handy, and she will feel a sense of worth.

Mastery orientation explains how individuals approach the tasks they have been given to do, and is similar to *explanatory style* insofar as there are two approaches to how people's attitude towards mastery influences their behaviour. In the first place there are helpless people, that believe that no matter what they do, their ability and level of autonomy don't allow them to take control and develop mastery of a specific task. They take life events personally and specific to them, they blame others for taking the wrong actions and their attribution choice point often leads them to blame the personality of others, and the locus of control of the situation is always external. These staff members need specific performance goals that can be checked off at the end of each day. They are wary of taking control of their own behaviours and prefer strong procedural guidelines to direct their behaviours. If something goes wrong they will be the first to abdicate responsibility and you will often hear *don't blame me, I just did what they told me to do.*

On the other hand, you may find mastery-oriented people. The mastery-oriented teacher will continuously try to find ways to improve their practice in order to reach a broader goal. They will experiment with innovative ways of achieving their goals, and once they have found a level of mastery, they are keen to share their good practice. These teachers and support staff see life events as general and not personal and when things go wrong they tend to look at their own reactions to a situation and learn from the failure. They have a very strong internal locus of control and constantly adjust their own efforts and persistence to improve what they are doing. The mastery-oriented individual needs outcomes-based goals and autonomy to follow whichever way works best to achieve mastery.

Turning Adequacy into Mastery

How can you predict how successful an initiative will be? Ultimately your aim with motivating staff is to turn *adequacy into mastery.* Before you spend a significant amount of time and money on a motivation program, or employing a performance coach to boost the outcomes of teaching and learning, you need to have some indication of how impactful such an initiative would be. There is, as with all human behaviour, no fool-proof way to determine the success of any program. If you set the stage so that the probability of success is high, then your school will benefit from the motivation program. You may start your preparation by getting to know the *mastery orientation* and *explanatory style* of your staff, as well as yourself. This will help you implement your knowledge and skills in motivation in order to achieve the vision you have set out for your school. In addition to understanding the attributional styles of your teachers and support staff, you should also consider:

☞ the ability (skills and knowledge) of staff to turn *adequacy into mastery.* What training is needed to improve the current situation?

☞ the effort that is typically exerted by teachers and staff as an inherent characteristic of the school's climate and culture. What changes in attitudes and behaviours are needed to turn *adequacy into mastery*?

☞ task-difficulty. How complicated and convoluted are the procedures that you are expecting teachers and support staff to follow? How can complexity be turned into simplicity?

☞ external impacts (community, socio-political and cultural influences). How do the strategic initiatives of the government and accountability structure help or hinder teachers and staff from turning *adequacy into mastery*?

Moving Towards Mastery

Once you have achieved clarity about the aspects of your school that needs further development, you can start thinking about a plan the changes that will motivate teachers and staff to turn their current level of performance into mastery. Included in your arsenal of strategies are peer-to-peer mentoring and coaching. Both strategies that are worth exploring in a school where there is a mix of experienced and new staff.

← new chapter.

Peer-to-peer Mentoring

As it is with all work settings, schools have members of staff that are either more experienced or more adept to change, mastery orientation and self-determination in regards to TLA strategies. You can make use of the existing skills within your school to set up a peer-mentoring program to support staff that find change and working towards mastery of TLA more challenging.

Peer mentoring has great potential when you want to develop and advance career growth and mastery of TLA behaviours. The aim of peer-to-peer mentoring is to co-facilitate the process from external regulation to identified regulation, and turn adequacy into mastery. The mentoring programme follows six distinct steps: pairing the mentoring dyad (pair), setting the mentoring goals, establishing the focus of the mentoring, negotiating the duration of the mentoring training of the mentor, and finally evaluating the progress of the mentoring sessions. The evaluation of the progress then serves to inform the setting or adjustment of the mentoring goals. It is important that there are no hierarchical differences between the co-mentors. The lack of seniority or hierarchy allows for easier communication, mutual support, and collaboration. The aim is not to manage the performance of teachers, but rather to develop an opportunity where teachers and support staff are encouraged to take risks by trying innovative strategies, where they are free and safe to discuss botched lessons and trial-run new ideas.

Characteristics of Peer-to-peer Mentoring

The first and most significant aspect of peer-to-peer mentoring is mutual trust. It's worth noting that it is best not to pair existing friends in a dyad. The reason for this is that despite the fact that trust is present between friends, sometimes the dyad will have to have difficult conversations, and the complications of having a friendship that expands beyond the periphery of the school gate, can unnecessarily complicate the dynamics of the peer-to-peer mentoring.

The second characteristic of peer-to-peer mentoring is that the dyad sets and sustains challenging expectations of one another. A sense of urgency to improve allows the dyad to hold each other to high expectations. This may even include an element of feeling the need to make the other proud of the personal and professional progress that is being made.

The third characteristic is that both members of the dyad benefit from the peer-to-peer mentoring program. Because there is no actual seniority, it is vital that the specific goal of the mentoring (as I will discuss a bit later) is decided on in such a way that both teachers feel that they are benefitting from these sessions. If one member of the dyad feels expendable or redundant, the mentoring will become a waste of time.

The fourth characteristic is that the relationship is not interdependent and exclusive. There is always an end date for the peer-to-peer mentoring. If the dyad starts to function in such a way that there is a co-dependency that develops, and the teachers cannot function without the mentor, then the main aim of facilitating a pathway towards identified regulation will not be reached.

The fifth characteristic of peer-to-peer mentoring is to maintain individual character traits. The dyad does not work in such close proximity that they adopt one another's relative traits. The relationship, although based on kindness and trust, remains a professional one. There must be an explicit expectation to set and achieve the specific goal. In other words, despite the fact that teachers, more than most other professions, gravitate towards making friends with other teachers, it is essential to know that the mentoring relationship has a specific reason. There is a distinctly stated goal, and that they will continuously evaluate and adjust their progress to remain on course towards achieving their targets.

The sixth characteristic of peer-to-peer mentoring is the visibility of the process. The mentoring process is overt, scheduled and in most cases, the majority of teachers and support staff either have access to such an initiative, or are obliged to participate in the mentoring program. It must be noted that not all teachers would be keen to involuntarily become part of a mentoring program, and it is more often than not better to provide the opportunity for teachers to participate and let the positive result speak for itself than making the peer-to-peer mentoring initiative mandatory.

The seventh characteristic of peer-to-peer mentoring is to base the relationship on coaching and role-modelling. Sharing good practice through peer observations, providing specific, positive, relevant and constructive feedback, and then trying the same TLA strategy again until the teacher feels personally satisfied with the results is part of the role-modelling loop. This leads to the final characteristic of internalising the peer-to-peer mentoring through *reflecting*, *reviewing* and *adjusting*.

Peer-to-peer Mentoring Steps

Step 1: Pairing of the Dyad, Needs Assessment and pre-training

You must remember the development needs of the teachers who will become a part of the peer-to-peer mentoring are. When pairing the dyad, it is critical to ensure that similar development needs are matched to provide a sense of continuance during the mentoring process. If the one teacher needs to improve her TLA practice and the other wants to pay specific attention to her assessment practice, there is a dissonance between which of the two goals is more important. This dissonance will, at best, leave the mentoring in a state of flux and, at worst, place your teachers at odds with one another. In addition, it might be wise to consider the professional compatibility of the dyad. Pairing two individuals who are both inclined to a negative explanatory style could render the process ineffectual from the start, in the same way, matching a dyad where a sense of overpowering and intimidating personality may overshadow a teacher with a timid disposition may cause anxiety, which in turn can make the workplace untenable for both of them. Because it isn't always easy to determine how individuals will react to peer-to-peer mentoring, it is vital that either party in the dyad can discontinue the peer-to-peer mentoring process without penalty or reprimand.

You must train the dyad in the specific policies relating to the particular goals, and they must be knowledgeable of the characteristics and process of mentoring. They should have additional training in practical and useful communication skills such as how to have difficult conversations without offending. This will ensure that the dyad enjoys the most effective impact of the mentoring program.

Step 2: Set Goals

The goals of the peer-to-peer mentoring program should be negotiated between the dyad and result in at least three stated and measurable outcomes. At the start, the goals may include explicitly stating the need to develop trust and understanding between the dyad. A second goal could consist of the specific development needs they have identified, and you can base the third on mastery of the particular need. These mentoring goals are continuously revisited to ensure the mentoring sessions stay on track. It is essential to state the specific success criteria for each goal at the very beginning of the goal setting session. You must be clear about the types of goals you expect your teachers to set before the mentoring program begins.

It is essential that you remember that trust forms a large part of developing a functioning mentoring relationship. However, you must also think about what impact such a relationship can have on each member of the dyad. You must ask yourself, at what point does trust become a burden of secrecy? At all times, the need for safeguarding must be kept in mind and you must be explicitly clear that the trust relationship between the dyad does not include where one party is concerned about safeguarding of students and staff. The goals that are set to improve practice should follow the SMARTER standard. In other words, the goals must be **s**pecific, **m**easu-rable, **a**pplicable, **r**ealistic, **t**ime-bound, **e**valuation must be done at particular waypoints, and **r**einforcement of desired behaviours must take place.

Step 3: Focus of Mentoring

It is crucial for the dyad to keep their mentoring sessions on track and focus on the goals that have been established in step 2. Mentoring, like life in general, follows a path of multi-finality – in other words, there is more than one path to develop the desired behaviours – and therefore the dyad has the flexibility to include emerging needs and issues that arise during the mentoring program. However, the dyad should be careful of adjusting the goals so frequently that the reason for the mentoring in the first place becomes forgotten. A specific time should be fixed for the mentoring meetings to help keep the focus on the mentoring. Peer-to-peer lesson observations, parallel assessment feedback, or cooperative lesson planning could also support them to achieve their goals.

Step 4: Duration and Place

Focus and sustainability are key words that informs the duration of the mentoring relationship. To be able to maintain attention on the mentoring sessions, an area that is away from the distractions that are typical of a school day must form the hub of the meetings. This is where your role as leader becomes essential. It is vitally important that the time for the mentoring to take place as well as the specific place (not in the classroom, staff room or other common areas) must be ring-fenced (protected time). If you plan the mentoring to start at the onset of the next academic year, you can set out a specific common-time in the dyad's timetable for mentoring. In addition, if there is the luxury of a spare room or more out of the way area where the privacy of the mentoring sessions can be respected, such an area must be specified and be protected from use by other staff or projects during the mentoring process. Each of the mentoring sessions should last no less than an hour, but the dyad must also consider that the mentoring does not take place in isolation from the rest of the TLA agenda of the school. Certain times of the year are busier than others: the pace of TLA is further increased by administrative duties, proctoring and other extra-curricular responsibilities. The dyad must be mindful that despite the importance of the mentoring process, life outside of the comfortable bubble of the dyad goes on.

Step 5: Mentoring Structure – The A to E of mentoring

Mentoring discussions can easily turn into a festival of complaining or mutually reinforced self-chastisement. It is therefore advisable to follow a structure during each of the meetings. I suggest that the following five points are used to help structure the mentoring meetings: Awareness, Beliefs, Challenges, Direction, and Exit Reflection. Each session should incorporate this A to E of mentoring

A core feature of peer-to-peer mentoring is not only developing one's *self-awareness* but also to improve one's *awareness* of the people and cues in the environment that may help to establish the effectiveness of teaching and learning. An example could be the student that comes into the class with a negative attitude, throws his books on the floor and fixes himself with defiance in his chair. It is easy to see that this is the beginning of a challenging lesson. However, if you have developed a sense of awareness you may realise why the student is in such a tempestuous mood. It will help you decide what actions to take to ensure that both you and he will benefit.

Your *beliefs* regarding the fundamentals of teaching and learning, assessment and student responsibility in the learning process will on both a conscious and subconscious level determine your TLA behaviours. If you don't believe that homework is effective, you will implement the school's homework policy with less than enthusiasm. Or if you believe that learning only takes place in isolation and complete silence, then that will be the expectation you have from your students, with the resulting conflicts that emanate from your attempts to establish such an environment.

Every situation where human interactions are the primary vehicle for development, such as the classroom, sports field or play area, comes with *challenges*. These challenges may be due to your areas for development, the pervasive climate in the school or even your feelings of inadequacy or frustrations relating to your private life. The fact is that TLA are filled with challenges. Being aware of, and honest about the challenges you face becomes one of the most critical aspects of the mentoring process. This is where you discuss best practice, next steps and *even better if* scenarios with your peer-mentor.

From the discussion regarding current and probable challenges, you aim to determine a new *direction* for the specific behaviour that will help you achieve the goals that you have set out at the beginning of the mentoring process. The direction goes hand-in-hand with specific behaviours that you will exercise for them to become embedded in your daily TLA practice. These behaviours may include taking specific action, implementing strategies, developing emotional control, improving on time management or implementing TLA initiatives.

Finally, an *exit reflection* places emphasis not only on what you have decided during the direction phase of the meeting, but also a reflection of the effectiveness of the meeting itself. Are there any things you would have wanted to discuss, or do you feel the relationship between you and your peer-mentor is established enough for a deeper sense of trust to become part of the process? What would you want to look at during the next meeting?

Step 6: Evaluation and Adjustment of Mentoring Programme

Continuous evaluation of the programme takes place on two levels: firstly, through *Exit Reflection* activity at the end of each session and secondly through continued communication between the dyad. You should determine specific waypoints at the onset of the mentoring process. These waypoints serve as indicators of how the process is progressing, and whether you should make any adjustments in time, place and focus. Most vitally, you will see if the mentoring is helping the dyad to improve. If the mentoring is perceived to be a waste of time, the dyad should look at the quality of the trust relationship, the structure of the meetings, the SMARTER goals and the activities that help the dyad improve their practice (such as peer observations, cooperative assessment and grading etc.). Some questions that may be beneficial during the process include:

- Does the mentee seem receptive to mentoring?
- How is communication between you and your mentee?

↝ What positive aspects have developed between you and your mentee?

↝ Are you satisfied with the scope the activities covered?

↝ Do you have any suggestions for additional activities?

↝ Is there any specific progress you think has been significant and should be celebrated and reinforced?

↝ Are there any special problems you would like to mention?

↝ Are there any "red flags" that say there may be trouble?

The autonomy, relatedness and competence that is fostered during the mentoring program lies at the heart of its success. As leader in the school, you do not receive feedback after the mentoring sessions, or even after the mentoring cycle has come to completion. The impact and success of the mentoring program is seen in the fruits that it bares - can you see mastery of TLA and most importantly, can you see an improvement in student progress levels?

Coaching

Some staff need more support. In some cases, peer-to-peer mentoring, performance management structures and formal punishers are less impactful than you would want them to be. However, the behaviour of the individual does not warrant suspension, a notice to improve or dismissal. Or, you may find that there is a dedicated and talented teacher who would benefit from individual coaching. In such cases performance coaching is a very good solution to consider.

Coaching is a long-standing legitimate form of skills development support that has been used to significant effect in the sporting arena. Translating the same role into the realm of TLA performance seems to be a natural step forward. Many teachers fulfil the role of coaching themselves during extramural activities whether on the sports field or in the debating club or on stage as the school play's director. Moreover, teachers and support staff often take on the role of an unofficial life coach in providing advice to, as well as a third-party view of a young person's skills, situation and experience. It is, therefore, a natural evolution to introduce the role of a coach into the personal and professional development of your teachers.

There is a significant difference between performance coaching and life coaching. Both look at the role of the coach to give the teacher an unbiased outside perspective. However, the life coach looks at the whole person (personal hopes and dreams, health, wealth and well-being) whereas the performance coach doesn't take into account the aspects of the teacher's life outside of her performance in the school.

From a humanistic perspective, personal well-being and performance are not mutually exclusive. You will find that your teachers, and rightly so, want to keep a dividing line between their work and private lives. However, when it comes to the psychology of human behaviour, such artificial lines do not exist. As a matter of fact, these two spheres of life are very much interdependent and one may argue that personal well-being and professional performance are the two side of the same coin. Based on this premise, it is best advised that you make use of the services of a professional life or skills coach.

Exit Reflection

Education by its very nature is magnanimous and selfless. It is not often that you will find a teacher that is in teaching for the money, and herein lies the problem facing leaders in education. Teachers tend to become spent at an alarming rate, running on stress inducing deadlines and auto-pilot for most of the year. Teachers that run on empty cannot be teachers that are in the process of developing mastery in teaching, learning and assessment, nor can they become intrinsically motivated and driven by self-determination.

Time, or rather the perceived lack of time, is the biggest barrier to excellence in education, and because accountability has proven to be a theme in education that is not going to go away soon (and nor should it), we have added yet another dimension to disempowering teachers. This is ironic, because the very construct of accountability implies that teachers should be empowered to be accountable for their TLA behaviours and strategies. Yet, through the nominal fallacy of the "prerequisite of control", distrust of teacher capacity and sense of purpose, as well as a lack of understanding of how self-determination works, school leaders tend to pile up the paperwork rather than streamline the system.

You should ask yourself:

- ✎ How are my actions and leadership behaviours empowerring or impeding teachers' development of self-determination?
- ✎ Do I feel in control of my own process of developing self-determination?

- ☞ What networks do I have access to , in order for my teachers to develop competency and relatedness?
- ☞ How am I fostering autonomy within my leadership team and among teachers and support staff?

VIII
POSITIVE PERFORMANCE MANAGEMENT

Performance management in education has always been a controversial subject to approach with teachers. While corporate environments have adopted qualitative measures to manage staff performance. It is much easier to measure whether sales targets have been met with a quantitative tool than it is to measure the value of a teacher's TLA contributions during learning. Therefore, teachers and some education leaders have maintained that the very nature of education requires a qualitative approach to evaluating teacher performance. Various accountability bodies across the globe have tried to marry qualitative descriptors with quantitative measures to satisfy those who insist on a measurable method and those who propose a descriptive approach.

Despite the apparent difficulty in implementing an effective performance management measuring tool, teachers in our bid to support our status as a chartered profession, must undergo a rigorous form of professional performance management. Continuous professional development targets, as well as performance related incentives, must form an integrated part of performance management. Not only does a clear performance management policy and implementation protocols encourage teachers to continuously improve their own TLA practices, it also provides a clear pathway for the school to move its provision of education towards achieving of mastery.

Performance management not only serves as a way to encourage personal accountability for TLA behaviours but also to instil a culture of forethought, self-reflection, self-regulation and self-determination across all spheres of the school environment. In the same way as students are encouraged to have a clear understanding of the pathway they have to follow to improve their academic progress, and how they are going to achieve their academic targets, teachers and support staff must have the same sense of direction and incentive to actualise their goals. It would be an interesting experiment to ask a random group of teachers what their TLA and pedagogical development goals are. I venture to say that many would admit that they do not have any.

That's why I propose implementing Positive Performance Management as a measuring tool for motivating teachers to work towards mastery of their craft.

Annual Positive Performance Management

Positive Performance Management (PPM) is based on the tenets of positive psychology. These include the beliefs that if conditions are right, we:

- 🖝 are mastery orientated;
- 🖝 yearn for self-determination (autonomy, relatedness and competency);
- 🖝 enjoy developing our competency;
- 🖝 are open to new experiences;
- 🖝 are inherently selfless.

Founded on our intrinsic need for self-actualisation and self-determination, PPM asserts that peak performance, peak experience, flow, relatedness, competency all lead to a greater sense of autonomy and mastery. Therefore, PPM does not call for financial or tangible rewards at the end of the PPM.

Based on these beliefs, PPM encourages individuals to take accountability for their own performance management by setting their own PPM targets, decide on what the outcome of each target should look like, and decide what evidence they will present in support of achieving their targets. Transparency and trust contributes to autonomy and relatedness and therefore the leadership of the school makes their efficiency growth plan as well as their personal leadership efficiency advancement and growth plane public. As a result, PPM encourages individuals to align their targets with the overall efficiency and growth of the school. During the PPM process a date for the performance management first review and final review is set. During the first review, individuals have the opportunity to state what is going well and make suggestions for changes to the PPM plan (Even Better If). These changes are agreed on, and at the final review a discussion about the PPM process, and to what extent targets have been achieved is agreed on.

Positive Performance Management Policy and Protocols

A clear performance management (PM) policy that is supported by protocols must be included in the leadership handbook and must include answers to the questions of why, who, when, where, and how.

Stakeholders in Positive Performance Management

There is a distinct need in education and among educators to have a performance management system that is transparent, democratic and free from leadership bias. In addition, in keeping with the tenets of self-determination, teachers prefer a system that is largely based on autonomy and individual competence, rather than statistics and quantitative measures. With this in mind, the stakeholders in Positive Performance Management are by and large removed from management structures and the role the leadership team plays is mostly administrative in nature.

PM Leader

The PM leader does not make any judgements regarding the performance of teachers and support staff. A process of nominating colleagues followed by a secret ballot should determine who the PM leader should be for a specific PM cycle. This position does not receive any incentive or contribute to any personal PM targets, and any member of staff can fulfil the post - I suggest that you should not include any members of the executive leadership team.

PM Line Manager

The PM Line manager serves as an advisor and administrator of the PM process. The PM line manager does not have to be the actual line manager of the member of staff or have any specific knowledge or understanding of the subject speciality of the teacher. You may decide that all middle leaders take on the role of PM line manager as part of their professional duties. The PM leader will allocate some staff members to each PM line manager, who in turn need to implement the PM protocols within the dedicated time frame.

PM Committee of Peers

The PM committee of peers consists of either elected, nominated or volunteer members of staff, and it makes up a vital part of the formal process of improving the school's capacity to grow. These individuals should be willing to contribute to the fairness of the PMP in a significant way. The PM committee of peers is not decided on or made public before the PM process starts insofar as their primary duty is to mediate and resolve disputes that may occur during the implementation of the PMP. If there are no disputes declared during the first phase of the PM process, no PM committee of peers is required. However, as soon as any staff member reports a disagreement, the PM leader will convene a committee of peers to contribute to the possible amelioration of such disputes. Thus, at any point during the PM process, a committee of peers can be convened and called into action.

The committee of peers can be convened either as representatives of specific individuals, as volunteers from the body of staff members or as nominated by staff members that are not part of the executive leadership team.

There are two possible ways to establish a committee of peers. Firstly, staff member should be able to apply to become a member of the committee of peers. The PM leader will consider the applications and choose members of the committee of peers to represent all members of the staff. Diversity, equality and inclusion should be considered at all times.

Secondly, staff can nominate peers at a whole staff meeting. A secret ballot should be conducted to establish who the representatives should be. The executive leadership team may nominate a non-voting member of the committee of peers to ensure that the committee has access to the correct information according to the school's policies and laws.

In the case where representatives of specific individuals is chosen, each individual that has declared a dispute (whether it is the staff member or the PM line manager) is allowed to nominate a peer to form part of the committee of peers. It is essential that an uneven number of peers are included to avoid deadlock situations when voting on possible resolutions. If there are too many potential applicants and nominees, the PM leader may choose a committee of 5 or 7 peers.

Even though the findings of the committee of peers cannot be made into policy or forced onto any party, the committee should take their duty serious enough that a win-win situation results from their findings and suggestions.

Role of Performance Management Leader

The PM leader oversees the implementation of the protocols, receives and reports concerns of teachers, union representatives and support staff to the executive leadership team. The PM leader manages the administrative aspects of setting the dates for PM protocols to be implemented, interim progress and adjustment discussion to take place and to conclude the final evaluation evidence and documentation. The PM leader collects all PM documentation on a specific date and passes these on to the executive leadership team for processing and safekeeping. During the interim evaluation and adjustment phase, the PM leader manages giving out and receiving documents to the appropriate parties.

- ☞ The PM leader receives declarations of dispute and arranges the implementation of protocols for disputes to be heard.
- ☞ The PM leader convenes a committee of peers that oversee disputes regarding the PM processes where PM discussions result in any disagreement.
- ☞ The PM leader conducts training with all stakeholders on the protocols of the PM process, including how to raise concerns and report complaints.

Essential Documents

It is perhaps unavoidable that paperwork and recordkeeping becomes part of the implementation of the PPM. In the perfect world we would have complete trust in technology to enter the brave world of paperless systems. However, it is expedient to ensure that records of the your teachers' goals and aspirations are kept secure. In order to minimise the amount of paperwork during the PPM process, we suggest only three documents should be included.

Efficiency and Growth Plan

The Efficiency and Growth Plan (EGP) is completed by the school's leadership team and sets out the vision and goals for the year ahead. The outcomes of this document are a School Vision Statement as well as the School Goals. Leaders will decide when and how they will measure the growth during the year and which non-financial incentives will be given to all stakeholders in the company.

Leadership Efficiency Advancement and Growth Plan

The Leadership Efficiency Advancement and Growth Plan (LEAGP) is in essence the performance management that the leadership team conducts on themselves. They evaluate their leadership efficacy and determine what they must do to grow their leadership competencies. These targets are made public to all stakeholders in the process of developing trust. The outcomes on this document includes School Efficiency Advancement Targets, Leadership Growth Target and Community Impact Target.

Individual Performance Target Plan

The Individual Performance Target Plan (IPTP), the first review and the final review encapsulates the individual's PPM experience. Individuals are asked to set their own targets, review dates and take accountability for being actively engaged in achieving these targets. There is no external management process other than the first and final reviews. The outcomes on these documents include: School Performance Target (this should be aligned with the Efficiency and Growth Plan), Personal Performance Target (based on the individual work development), Career Development Target (CPD, courses, affiliations and conferences), Personal Health Target (if you are healthy, you will be more efficient at work, happier at home and feel a stronger sense of fulfilment) and finally a Community Service Target (community service leads to a more significant sense of gratitude).

Implementation of the Positive Performance Management Program

At the beginning of the year, the leadership team completes the LEAGP and then facilitates individual meetings with staff. The climate and culture surrounding PPM is one of trust and the understanding that if the leadership takes care of their team, the team will take care of the customers. Staff members receive the completed EGP and LEAGP and an empty IPTP document prior to meeting in order to decide on their targets, outcomes and evidence. During the planning meeting with individuals a first review and final review dates are determined. It is good practice to provide some indication in the yearly calendar when these will happen and it is the responsibility of the leadership team to ensure that the review and final review dates are kept open and not moved.

Performance Management Protocols

There are five aspects of the positive performance management protocols that need to be included into you PM policy and protocols document: target setting, sources of evidence, interim progress evaluation and adjustment, and the final evaluation followed by next steps.

197

Target Setting

Target setting is the most fundamental part of any successful PM process. It is vital that teachers explicitly state their targets and to attached clear descriptions of their expected outcomes to each of the stated targets. Performance management targets must also include the development of the whole person. Similarly, targets should not only focus on one or two professional development or TLA related aspects of where the executive leadership team feels improvement is needed. As a matter of fact, the process of target setting requires from the teachers and staff members to consider their own areas for development and take accountability for where they need to improve.

Each cycle of PM includes setting five personal targets as well as the related expected outcomes of each target. The line manager will record the targets for each of the five targets, after a discussion with the teacher on the provided protocol documents. Targets should include:

To encourage teachers and support staff to be accountable for their personal, professional development and TLA behaviours, it is important to also allow them self-determination over their progress. This can, of course, lead to situations where a member of staff doesn't consider the PM protocols to be as serious as one would want them to and provide targets that are not in line with achieving mastery in education. In such a case either party can declare a dispute through the PM leader.

TLA/ Professional Duties Target

This target is directly related to the TLA/professional duties of the staff member. You may wish to provide suggestions of TLA actions that have been identified as whole school priorities. However, you should not prohibit staff from choosing their own TLA targets. In general, teachers should decide which aspect of their TLA practice needs to move from adequacy to mastery. In order to do this, teachers must feel safe to honestly reflect on their own practice and be open about their areas for development. However, your school might have started on its journey from adequacy to mastery, in which case teachers will not merely set a target to improve aspects of their practice, but rather actively look for areas where they are already good, but want to become master practitioners.

Whole-school Development Target

You should think about the whole-school priorities that you have decided on and create a list of up to five priorities that can be highlighted on the individual performance target plan. Staff can choose their whole school development target from this list of whole school priorities according to the annual school improvement plan. Staff members should identify an area where they feel they can make a significant difference or contribute to the school's improvement according to their strengths. Aspiring leaders should consider these targets as a way to advance their emerging leadership skills. Examples could include becoming part of working parties, select committees, TLA research groups, conducting training and workshops to groups of teachers or support staff as well as being a mentor for new staff members. The options and possibilities should be considered and discussed prior to the PM process starts, however that doesn't mean that innovative suggestions by staff should not be considered.

Continuous Professional Development Target

Each staff member must identify an area where they feel CPD training could benefit their own professional development. In order to streamline the CPD provision process, you can provide teachers and staff with specific focus areas from which they can choose. However, you should not prohibit a teacher or member of the support staff from finding CPD courses and providers that suit their development needs. Insofar as there are clear budget implications for encouraging staff to engage in CPD you may wish to limit the amount of money each member of staff is allocated for CPD. You may also want to negotiate price reductions through CPD providers and provide a list of these providers to teachers and support staff. However, you should be open to negotiating part funding of additional qualifications through higher education institutions with staff. Finally, you may consider what your policy regarding rolling financing over to the next financial year, before you discuss CPD funding with staff. In the case where a member of staff considers a multi-year qualification, you should allow appropriate interim outcomes to serve as a measurement of success. For example, you may feel that having passed the relevant modules of a postgraduate diploma as a pertinent outcome at the end of the year even though they have not completed the course yet.

Personal Health Target

The physical and mental health of your teachers and support staff are some of the most important aspects of leading your school to become exceptional in its education outcomes. Not only does a healthy workforce save you money, but it also ensures that your teachers and support staff can fulfil their duties with more energy, enthusiasm, optimism and verve. It is therefore important that you include a personal health target into the PM mix. These can often be highly personal, and PM line managers and staff should use their own discretion as to which targets to include and how to measure the success of these target. An example of such a personal health target could range from joining a walking club and providing proof of participating in at least five walking events over the duration of the year, to joining a book club and providing proof of attending the majority of book club meetings over the span of the year.

Personal health targets can be completely outside of the box, for example a teacher may decide that he will spend at least one hour a week at a trampoline jumping park with his children, providing that the parent has the ticket stumps that includes the "admit one adult" or some selfies to prove that he actively participated as evidence, there is no reason that such family bonding and activities should not be allowed as personal health targets.

It is important that you, the PM leader as well as all staff take this target as seriously as the TLA and CPD targets: happy teachers make for happy students, and happy students show exceptional progress.

Community Service Target

We learn through seeing and experiencing, and if the school's over-arching vision is to facilitate its young people to become responsible members of a growing society, then it is essential to show them what responsible citizenry consists of. In the same way as the personal health target should be considered as a vital aspect of the PM process, community service should receive specific importance. Again, the staff member's own choice comes into play; however, you may wish to allow staff to choose to become actively involved in the school's selected charity events, or become actively involved their chosen charities or community support. It is also worth stating that there is an additional benefit to having staff being seen doing community service or working for a charity, is that your students can learn by example. Similarly it strengthens the school's moral imperative as a bastion of social development in the eyes of the local school community.

Another added benefit is that a member of staff can participate in community service as a family activity, which encourages teachers and support staff to spend productive and positive time with their families. You should make it clear to your teachers that making a donation to a charity does not constitute being actively involved in a charity or community support, and donating money or goods cannot be accepted as evidence for achieving this target.

After the targets, related outcomes and success criteria, sources of evidence and possible mitigating circumstances have been agreed both the PM line manager and the staff member immediately dates and signs the document in front of one another. If either one of the parties declines to sign, there should be no further discussion or questions, and a dispute is automatically declared without anyone having to give reasons for their decision.

The recording and documenting of the chosen five targets, their related outcomes, the possible sources of evidence, interim progress evaluation and agreed adjustments to outcomes and evidence can be drawn up as you find fit. However, because these documents will play a significant role in the executive leadership team's decisions to reward teachers and support staff, they are considered as legal and contractual documents, and you should deal with these papers with the same sense of security and importance as all legal documents. At the end of the PM cycle, you should add the relevant records to the staff files to serve as evidence of professional progress and competency.

Evidence

The performance management protocols include the expectation that teachers and support staff provide evidence of the outcomes they achieved. Evidence for the TLA and profession-nal duties target will usually be based on observation by a member of the leadership team, scrutiny of student work or recorded student progress data. It is vital that you decide on which the specific forms of evidence and what a successful outcome will look like, from the onset of the targets setting process.

The discussion between the PM line manager and the staff member will include how realistic the predetermined expected outcomes are, what range of success will be acceptable and which mitigating circumstances you will accept when discussing the results. For example, if a teacher's target is to have all her students show progress during the academic year, the line manager may suggest that they should consider changing the goal to no less than 90% of students should show appropriate progress over time.

You could implement a RAG system to help determine progress of learning. RAG stands for Red, Amber and Green. Students that have shown a regression in their progress are coded as Red, students that have made no progress are coded as Amber and students that have made good progress are coded as Green. Following this RAG system students that are highlighted with amber and green for progress will be considered as showing progress. As a mitigating circumstance, you will not include students who have come into the year group after a specific date when in measuring the outcomes.

Evidence for the actualisation of the whole-school development target will include the success parameters that are indicated in the school improvement plan, and evidence can range from relevant recorded data to achieved outcome descriptors. Because whole-school targets are often spread across several years, you may suggest that the teacher writes a list of actions taken or describes their active participation in a short paragraph as evidence. Because it is easy to verify participation in committees and working groups, such descriptions should suffice as evidence.

Training providers often issue certificates of attendance or the relevant professional bodies that teachers belong to may have a points system that can serve as evidence CPD participation. In the case where you consider a postgraduate diploma or other higher education qualification, that spans over several years, the academic transcripts or assessor's feedback on modules passed should be acceptable evidence of progress towards achieving the qualification.

Evidence for personal health and community service can be varied and range from a thank you letter from the administration of the local Hospice or Care Home to a report from the local newspaper or blog in which the community service is chronicled. A medal for the completion of a walkathon or similar events can suffice as evidence of personal health targets being reached.

Interim Progress Evaluation and Adjustment

Schools are dynamic environments that are subject to change, often without prior warning. In the same way, performance management is far from an exact science. Thus, it is expedient to anticipate that modifications to the PM targets, outcome specifications or envisaged evidence could come into play. Also, once the school year has started in earnest and the first assessment deadlines start to loom, the last thing on any teacher's mind is the PM targets and related evidence gathering. The interim progress evaluation, therefore, has a dual purpose. The first is to remind teachers and support staff to keep in mind that PM is applicable throughout the academic year. The second is to allow teachers and support staff to self-reflect on the targets and outcomes they have set and to adjust either the targets, related outcomes or the evidence that is needed during the final evaluation. The PM leader should determine dates of this mid-point evaluation and ensure that all members of staff have the opportunity to have a progress discussion with their PM line manager.

Final Evaluation and Next Steps

The final review of the PM process takes place during a third meeting between the PM line manager and the staff member. The staff member would have received a copy of their targets document at least two weeks before this meeting to have ample time to gather and collate evidence. During the meeting, the staff member presents his/her evidence, and after a discussion where the evidence and the success criteria (that the staff member has determined themselves during the first meeting) is evaluated, each target is marked as either, fully achieved, emergent or not achieved. If there is agreement both parties sign the document which is taken to the PM leader by the PM line manager. If there is no agreement, the staff member does not sign the report, which automatically declares a dispute, which will be followed up by the PM leader in due course.

Quantifying the outcome of the PPM process should not become a complicated process. Each target receives either two points for being "fully achieved", one point for "emerging" and null points for "not achieved". At the end of the final evaluation discussion with the PM line manager, the calculate the total points to indicate the outcome of the PMP. The PM leader then records this point and submitted to the executive leadership team. The PM policy should determine how incentives, rewards and increments on annual remuneration should be considered. The PM point may be one of several aspects that the executive leadership team takes into account when they determine whether a teacher or support staff member becomes eligible for an increment, or it could be the sole indicator. Whichever way, it is essential that the PM point plays a significant role in determining incentives, pay progression and rewards.

The PPM process includes strong elements of self-determination. PM leader, is a peer and does not form part of the executive leadership team's agenda. This impartiality makes the PMP much more reliable and objective.

Declaration of Dispute Protocols

If a dispute is declared, the PM line manager will discuss her/his concern that the targets are not of adequate valence to ensure that the staff member makes significant professional progress in his/her TLA or professional practice. If there is no agreement regarding the personal targets, either the PM line manager or member of staff can declare a dispute through the PM leader, which in turn will be evaluate by a committee of peers. The committee of peers will make recommendations in order to find agreement. If the recommendations are not to the satisfaction of either party, an appeals process can be taken to the governing body of the school or the relevant teacher and support staff union procedures can be followed.

Disputes are automatically declared when a staff member or PM line manager declines to sign the relevant documents. No forms need to be filled in, nor do either party have to explain during the target setting, interim evaluation or final evaluation why they are declaring a dispute. Recognition of the dispute is formally communicated to both parties in writing within one week of the PM meeting.

The dispute must be recorded and after the PM process has been completed, both parties are invited to write a short declaration of why they wish to declare a dispute. Receipt of the declaration is formally record and handed over to the PM committee of peers within a week of recognising the declaration of the dispute. To minimise the impact on staff morale and stress related to the PM dispute, the PM committee of peers must convene and resolve all cases within a total of three weeks of the end of the PM process.

It is the right of any person who has declared a dispute to appeal the decision of the committee of peers. This appeal will be handled by the executive leadership team with oversight by the school's governing body.

Rewards and Incentives

Remuneration, annual increments and salary structures are technically incentives that are given in exchange for motivation. The staff member is *motivated* to get up in the morning and come to work, to fulfil the minimum duties according to the employment contract and job description and in exchange, s/he receives her salary. However, these motivators are in most cases determined by the laws of the land and you have little control over it except for maybe deciding what annual increment is applicable. The incentives and rewards you do have power over have much lesser monitory value, yet concerning personal value, staff may attach particular significance to them.

Remember, that for a reward to be of motivational value, there must be expectancy-value in it. In other words, it must be sure that a bonus or incentive can be received, the incentive must be of personal value and should be pleasant, and the individuals must know that the attached goal is achievable.

Exit Reflection

Despite all the incentive programs and rewards schemes, research has found that recognition, the simple act of acknowledging in public the contribution and effort a staff member has contributed to a project or common goal is the most influential external motivator you as a leader has. There is a catch though. If the praise is not warranted, and it is predictable that everybody, notwithstanding their level of contribution or success will receive this public acknowledgement, then it renders the public praise sterile. For instance, the blanket *we want to thank everybody, but there is not the time to mention their names* or the anonymous *thank you all, you know who you are*, are ineffective and lazy leadership at best. If your teachers and support staff made the time to contribute to your vision, you should make the time to acknowledge them by name, and in public.

The policy of **"praise in public and punish in private"** should permeate the entire school, from the very top where the governors monitor the efficacy and progress of the whole school too, leadership structures, teachers and support staff right to the individual custodial worker that reminds students to pick up their litter.

In this chapter you have learned:

- ☞ how to allow teacher and support staff to make use of a democratic process of performance management;
- ☞ how to use the tenets of positive psychology and self-determination to increase teacher engagement and purpose;
- ☞ how to design and implement a positive performance management program;
- ☞ how to deal with disputes during the performance management process;
- ☞ that you should always praise in public and punish in private.

IX

DECISION-MAKING STYLES

Whether in the classroom or in the meeting room, leadership boils down to how you make decisions, and how you take responsibility and stand accountable for your choices. For you to develop and cultivate your leadership skills to be most effective you need to gain an understanding of how leaders make decisions and what the most effective decision-making style is.

Each individual has a decision-making style that influences the way and the type of decisions s/he makes. Throughout this chapter, you will identify what your decision-making style is and develop the tools to help you use your specific style to make the best possible choices for your school and in your classroom. You will also learn how to use your understanding of the decision-making styles of the teachers and education leaders you work with to reach the best possible outcomes for all your students.

Making decisions is a not an exact science and making effective choices, even less so. There just isn't any fool-proof way of ensuring that you have covered all the bases, that you have thought about all the variables or that the weather will play along with your plans. Individuals have an integrated tendency towards making decisions which have developed alongside and in the same way as personal attributes. As integrated as your personality, your human agency, your locus of control, and your explanatory style is to your behaviour, so too is your decision-making style. As a leader in education, your self-awareness of your own decision-making style is as necessary as your understanding of how the decision-making style of your teachers, students and support staff influences their choices and behaviour.

As teacher and school leader you often have to make on the spot decisions, without any careful forethought or deliberation. When you think about some situations, during which you have had to make an on-the-spot decision, you have most certainly asked yourself, why you or others have made that specific decision? What were their intentions, or did they merely react to the situation. When you think about the verb *decide,* it conjures up a process, a deliberate and conscious act of cognition. Even the fact that it is a verb, a *doing word,* suggests that it follows a course, yet when we take a look at our own experience we realise that this is not always true. Deciding isn't always a deliberate action. To the contrary, sometimes making a decision or choice seems to be automatic and immediate.

Even when you endeavour to deliberately make considered and rational choices, the unconscious mechanisms of decision-making tend to determine how you will feel about, and the confidence you have in the decisions you have made. If you examine your decision-making process, you have to consider your thinking processes, and this includes unconscious thinking. From an understanding of how the unconscious mind works, it is clear that a more profound unconscious mechanism is at work in the decision-making process and that even though it didn't seem like we were actively deciding, our integrated decision-making style did the choosing for us. To understand how decision-making can be an automatic "style of thinking", we have to havew a better idea of how thinking works. In the following section, we look at the conscious and unconscious mind, and how the human brain is continually making decisions without us being aware of it.

The Unconscious Mind at Work

Psychologists and neurologists have been exploring the human decision-making process for several decades. From Freud to Kahneman we see that our understanding of the human thinking process and thus the human decision-making process is increasing on a daily basis. Every day we find out more and more about how our brains function and how we make decisions.

Thinking and decision-making are inextricably linked. The one cannot go without the other, yet looking at geo-economic and political events, it is difficult to imagine that a rational decision-making process lies behind many of the choices some leaders make.

Daniel Kahneman and Amos Tversky, two of the world's leading thinkers about thinking, explain that thought takes place on two plains: the conscious, or knowing mind, and the unconscious, or unknowing mind. The concept of unconscious *thinking* seems like a contradiction in terms, yet when we reflect more closely about the unconscious mind, we realise that this unobserved world of thinking plays a significant part in how and why people decide to do things. Unconscious thinking drives your immediate response to a situation: you are often aware of the thoughts that are milling at the back your mind, but not the reason why you react in a specific way. Whereas your unconscious thoughts take the form of ideas and understanding, our conscious thoughts take the form of words and sentences - even punctuation. Our decision-making processes works in more or less the same way as your conscious and unconscious thoughts do.

There are six aspects of the unconscious mind that are important when we consider how decision-making works:
a) unconscious thoughts do not occur in words, but rather in clusters of ideas, metaphors, constructs of understanding, emotions, skills and perceptions;
b) unconscious thoughts are learned from previous experiences and when we remember experiences they have an automatic and immediate impact on how we *decide* to react;
c) unconscious thoughts allow us introspection after behaviour but not while the behaviour is taking place;
d) unconscious thinking is not good at making rational choices that are based on what is right and wise, it is instead based on emotions and preferences;
e) unconscious thoughts are ever-present, although we are not always aware of them;

f) unconscious thoughts are continually looking out for aspects of the world around you that are related to the problem or matters on your mind; and

g) finally, unconscious thoughts are compelling, and they influence *what* we decide to do in the end.

Theoretical Perspectives From a Previous Era

To develop a clearer understanding of what we already know of how we decide, it is important to review some of the established decision-making theories of the previous century. As you have seen above, psychologists, economists and neurologists have been at the spearhead of research on how decisions are made and with the recent development of fMRI technology, neurologists have been able to map the human brain, including how and where we make decisions. I have included four decision-making theories that may contribute to your understanding of decision-making as a whole. These are game theory, rational choice, bounded rationality and moral decision-making theory.

Game Theory

Game Theory is a decision-making theory that suggests that we don't ever make choices in isolation, but rather that we are players in *a game*, and that we make specific decisions to secure the most beneficial outcome from a situation. Based on this theory, there are winners and losers in any decision that is made, and whichever decisions one player makes, this decision influences other choices s/he, as well as other people, will make. The decision can be cooperative or non-cooperative. In cases where decision-makers cooperate with each other, we can observe a mutually beneficial outcome which may or may not be the best one. If the decision is non-cooperative and where one player may be better off by cheating, then usually both players tend to *cheat*, and neither decision-makers get what they wanted. In such a case, it makes sense to approach a decision from a position of cooperation or negotiation, however in a world where one dog often eats another, a *"winner takes it all"* approach might be most beneficial to the individual. This approach leaves us with the situation where inequality becomes prevalent. Game Theory predicts the outcomes of situations where social norms provide us with restrictive rules that show us what is permitted, expected or forbidden. These social norms also influence the autonomy of choice we have. However, in Game Theory, there are no winners from *cheating* behaviour. Nevertheless, if they repeat the game, the decision-makers are likely to act rationally and avoid conflicts with each other.

Rational Choice Theory

The second way of looking at the anatomy of decision-making comes from the field of economics in the guise of Rational Choice Theory. Even though some people think of reason and rationality as synonymous, it is essential to distinguish between these two ideas. What we usually consider as sensible, logical and sound judgment (rational) isn't necessarily what economists suggest when they talk about rational agents. In Rational Choice Theory, a rational agent is first and foremost self-interested.

A rational choice will be one where one's personal benefit is maximised. We make decisions by thinking about the probability of an event and calculating the value of each possible outcome. Then we multiply these two values by each other to calculate the expected benefit. Let's say event A could happen with a probability of 0.9 and will have a reward to the value of 2. The predicted benefit equation might merely look like 0.9 x 2 = 1.8. Another event, event B could happen by a probability factor of 0.1 and will have a reward to the value of 20. Here the benefit equation might simply look like 0.1 x 20 = 2. Thus, according to rational choice theory, you would go with decision B because its expected value is larger than A and therefore it will be more beneficial to you (2 > 1.8). However, the rational choice from a personal perspective does not necessarily imply a rational decision from a societal perspective.

An example of this is to look at the banking crisis of 2008. Right before the mortgage crisis started, financial institutions around the world were paying enormous amounts of money as bonuses to their top-traders. Due to this bonus-based compensation scheme, the traders, bankers, and almost every decision-maker involved in the financial industry were taking excessive risks, beyond their means. According to rational choice theory, this was rational behaviour. Nevertheless, it was not a time when sensible, logical and sound judgments were in action. As a result, we all experienced a global financial crisis that changed the world. To place rational choice theory in context of your day-to-day activities at school, you should ask yourself, if the behaviour of a member of staff or student, however selfish you may think it is, could be seen as rational – keeping in mind that rational responses do not necessarily imply, ethical, moral, or logical behaviour.

Bounded Rationality

Bounded Rationality is the third perspective that influences our way of understanding decision-making. The theory of bounded rationality proposes that the *limits of rationality* confine us, and thus, decision-makers can only make choices based on the information they have. The theory places further emphasis on the limitations of an individual's rational decision-making skills by looking at what restrictions s/he may face, such as critical thinking skills, capability in the field where s/he has to make a decision, Values and knowledge.

There are three particular limitations every decision maker has to face. Firstly, we often possess over limited and unreliable in-formation regarding any of the possible alternative options. Secondly, as humans, our conscious mind has a limited capacity to analyse, evaluate and come to a conclusion about the choices to make. Thirdly, time places a restraint on the decision-making process. In the most complex situations, this usually leads a person to make satisfying decisions rather than maximum impact decisions. In simpler terms, the extent to which we can make a rational decision is directly linked to the information, thinking capacity (you may venture to say intelligence) and time constraints we face when we are making any decision. This means that more often than not, *decisions are based on a good-to-fit rather than a best-to-fit basis.*

There are two different forms of rationality that we should consider before we move on: substantive rationality and procedural rationality. In the first instance, a leader makes a substantively rational decision if she has clear criteria of what successful outcomes should be, and if she does not give up working towards achieving these outcomes until she has met the specific requirements. In such a case, she has made a substantive rational decision not to give up. In applied leadership, this supports the principle of setting a clear vision, backed by unambiguous goals. If you know where you want to take your school and you know what the outcomes will look like when you *get there*, you will be able to make substantive rational decisions.

However, for a leader to be procedurally rational, the decision can only be made after an appropriate process of deliberation, discussion, reflection and contingency planning that is related to how important she thinks the problem is itself. In school leadership terms, the leader designs and implements the process and policies before the encountering problem. That means that you will make decisions according to the pre-proposed procedures. However, no vision or goals are needed for the leader to make rational procedural choices. This form of decision-making is the most common in education, and may more often than not be the cause of dispassionate relationships, unhappiness and detachment from the human part of teaching and learning. The more positive side of the coin is that procedural rationality tends to be more fair, objective and free from personal bias than substantive rational decision-making.

Moral Decision-making

The fourth approach to understanding how we make decisions is moral decision-making: how we tell *right* from *wrong*. At this point, I wish to note that the cultural indicators that guide what is considered to be right or wrong are a conversation worth much more time than I can afford in this chapter. However, it is vital to note that looking at how culture impacts on the decision-making process is worth further investigation and may contribute to a deeper understanding of why leaders in education behave in specific ways. The importance of moral decision-making is most evident when we compare it to the previous two approaches. Both game theory and rational choice theory place emphasis on the best personal gain a decision will bring. Moral decision-making binds these together and emphasises the impact of your choices on your school community and society as a whole. Without considering the effect of your decisions on the people around you, pretty soon a *dog-eat-dog world* will have no dogs left to eat.

Morality is a touchy subject. Not only do we have to consider the culture, religious and rights characteristics of our moral values, we also have to admit that our intuition and self-serving bias have an influence on how and what we decide. We are subject to personal biases, and on-the-spot morality isn't the most straightforward approach to making decisions. As a leader in education, it is your responsibility to have clarity on your values positions and the ethical boundaries that you have set for yourself. Besides, morality or morals-based decisions often provoke strong emotional reactions. It is usually most com-fortable to try not to walk blindly into the mine-field of debate on morals when we make decisions, however, because we primarily build schools on the moral imperatives of rights, social justice and social mobility, it is not so easy to try and avoid the ethical dimensions of your decisions.

From a behavioural perspective, researchers are still exploring how different decision-making styles and approaches influence the economic, political and social spheres of society. You could link such decision-making styles to underlying in-person characteristics and cognitive styles that are *unique self-consistencies in information processing that develop congenial ways around underlying personality trends*. In other words, when you decide to take a specific course of action, the process in which you choose falls on a spectrum from probability reasoning, (*if* this happens, *then* I will do that), to an audit of cost and benefits (rational choices). The way you make decisions don't always fall on one side of the spectrum or the other; it often depends on the situation, context and value/importance you link to the decision, where on the spectrum our decision-making style falls.

Dimensions of the Relative Decision-making Model

According to the relative decision-making model, there are six dimensions, that each function on a continuum, and play an important role in the way we make decisions. These are reasoning, acuity, decision autonomy, openness to experience, control patterns and emotions. Your decision-making style depends on where you fall on the spectrum of each of these dimensions.

The first dimension is reasoning: in other words the conscious and deliberate thinking about the variables that come into play when you have to make a decision. The reasoning continuum ranges from rational decision-making, where on the one side of the continuum you have to weigh up the costs and benefits of a choice, and on the other hand the potential or possibility-based approach.

The second dimension of decision-making explores the individual's acuity (alertness and perception). In short, your acuity functions within the context of your environment and in decision-making it exists on a continuum from analytical acuity to intuitive acuity. The reasoning continuum and the acuity continuum go hand-in-hand, like being in a close orbit when considering your decision-making style.

The third dimension of decision-making styles is decision autonomy. This feature explores your perceived freedom, self-reliance and self-determination to make decisions. Here you will ask yourself whether you think you have the authority to make a decision; whether you like making decisions, or whether you feel confident in your ability to make decisions? Autonomy falls on a range from high decision-autonomy to low decision-autonomy, and this has a significant impact on your decision-making style.

The fourth dimension of decision-making involves your openness to experience. On the continuum of openness to experience, your preference will either have a propensity towards being curious and inquisitive, or you will feel more comfortable to make cautious and careful choices. In the fifth place, control patterns explore your locus of control. The continuum of control patterns ranges from external-reactive to an internal proactive locus of control.

The final dimension considers the impact of emotions on your decision-making process. Control patterns and feelings, in the same way as reasoning and acuity, are bound in a closed path and cannot be seen as mutually exclusive in determining the style with which you make decisions. The emotion continuum ranges from emotion dependent to emotion neutral. In other words, on the one side, emotions play a substantial part in how you decide and on the opposite side, you are emotionally neutral when you choose.

Reasoning

Reasoning, also known as the process of thinking about the decision, forms the first dimension on which you base your decision-making. Reasoning falls on the *rational – potential/possibility-based* continuum. Commonly, you might prefer a reasoning processes that *favours stability over change*, and the main reason for thinking, or reasoning, about a decision, is to avoid risk. In the school setting, especially when safeguarding is considered, risk avoidance is the highest priority.

The overall value of an option is given by the balance of its advantages and its disadvantages. In other words, a cost/benefit-based approach will look at how a specific decision will yield the highest benefits. A rational approach to risk avoidance is to plan, to set policies and procedures in place, to disseminate the policies and procedures and to hold teachers, students and support staff accountable for keeping to the *letter of the law.* No deviation from the proceedings is allowed, and when you conduct whole-school inspections or class visits, you will have a clear set of criteria that are either present or not. This is very much a *tick box* approach of decision-making.

When we compare the cost of a decision with how much we expect to win in the end, it seems like an efficient way of making a decision. The problem with creating seemingly intelligent predetermined lists of the benefits and disadvantages of choice is our distinct lack of clairvoyance because we live within the confounds of bounded rationality. Despite our ability to recognise trends and know our weaknesses, it is virtually impossible to see all the variables that will make it possible to avoid all forms of risk. Pre-determined policies and procedures may be rational, objective, fair and democratic, however, on the very opposite side of a rational decision-making spectrum is inflexibility, not recognizing the human factor and you may even be accused of being cold or unfair.

On the other hand, the potential/possibility-based approach is much more flexible, and even though contingency plans may be in place, if you fall on this end of the continuum, you will feel comfortable to make decisions on the go, solving problems and taking opportunities as they come along. How often do we find ourselves making a decision based on the probability of an event taking place? Does *if it rains tonight, I will not wash the car* sound familiar to you? The choice to wash the car might seem like an insignificant decision, however, if you think about how decisions are made in schools, making significant decisions about how to avoid risks at school, how to improve TLA or even of addressing issues such as rewards and punishment in your school is not unheard. Prospective decision-making is based on the perceived likelihood of an event or events taking place.

We often don't know the full extent of probability of something happening, or how a project will play out, yet we have a vague notion of the likelihood of an event taking place. We often make decisions with the foreknowledge of what the consequences may entail, and making *choices under uncertainty requires that we reflect on the appeal of the possible outcomes and the prospect of it happening*. We often face ambiguity, and it is difficult to determine all the variables we have to think about when we choose. This contributes to us feeling that we have to *wait and see* before we can decide. Yet, our innate tendency to avoid risk drives us to predict prospective outcomes. Keep in mind, your personal preferences and beliefs also play a significant part in your decision-making process. When making a decision, an event has more bearing on an individual choice when that situation turns impossibility into a possibility and then into probability. Combine this with the sheer number of choices we deal with on a daily basis, it is no wonder some people feel anxious about making decisions.

Acuity

No person is an island. We all function within the boundaries of our communities and society as a whole, and the interactions and interpersonal relationships we have within our community have an impact on our behaviours, beliefs, as well as the processes of our conscious and unconscious minds. Acuity is the accumulative awareness of your environment, which in turn shapes the way in which you make decisions. In other words, no matter how well we plan, unforeseen events will take place, and problems will occur in any situation. One of the reasons you are expected to make decisions is to prevent or solve such problems. Acuity, as part of the decision-making process, looks at how aware you are of issues that may occur (or that have already happened), and your acuity helps you to think about how to prevent or solve such problems.

On the continuum of acuity, we find on the one side an analytical acuity which follows a systematic method of identifying and finding solutions for problems. If you have an analytical acuity, you tend to look at small details, and you prefer to the step-by-step analysis of events. You have a natural preference for recognising patterns in technical and procedural information that may influence how you decide to approach a problem. On the other side of the continuum, we have intuitive acuity. The easiest way to explain intuition is the act of thinking without rational inference. In other words, that feeling you get in the back of your head that warns you that something is wrong, or the sense you have that what you are doing is right, you just don't know how to explain why you think so. Intuition is *a way of learning that takes place beyond consciousness, in which a decision-maker acquires knowledge, but is unable to identify the source of this* experience.

Your personality attributes, abilities and beliefs, in conjunction with the school, the culture and the socio-political climate you grew up and developed in all have an impact on how you learn to react at any decision point.

Human intuition is an evolutionary device that has secured our species to flourish, especially when it comes to our young, thus, even if you prefer an analytical approach to problem-solving, your intuition will always play a role in how you make decisions, and should be ignored at your peril. Intuition is not the opposite of logic, nor is it based on irrational actions. Your unconscious mind is responsible for providing you with a "deeper" knowledge, which is based on experiences you have gathered over a lifetime. Your intuition forms an integral part of any decision-making process mainly through an automatic inductive process, which helps to increase the accuracy and effectiveness of the decision-making process.

Individuals seldom depend exclusively on analytical or intuitive acuity in the decision-making process. A teacher's intuition is often one of her abilities that has developed the strongest, especially when it comes to safeguarding our students and recognizing patterns of neglect.

Decision Autonomy

Having *your say*, your freedom of speech and having decision-making power over your body are some of the fundamental human rights that form part of your *right to freedom*. However, some theorists suggest that we don't have any freedom (autonomy) in our lives; that our destinies are determined by the ruling or governing classes; and that freedom to make our own decisions, is severely restricted. Some philosophers suggest that free will doesn't exist at all. The freedom to decide is one of the most problematic aspects of decision-making. As humans, we have an innate human agency – the inborn capacity to make choices. The core features of human agency include our intentions (proactive commitment) to bring about future actions or decisions; our forethought (action plan) and how we aim to deal with likely consequences of decisions; self-reflectiveness which includes the motivation and our self-regulation to uphold our course of action and estimation of our progress in order to achieve the predetermined goals; and finally the ability (through self-reflectiveness) to evaluate how productive our capacity for control is. However, in a complex society, with rules, laws and codes of conduct, we don't always have the freedom to make the choices we want to.

We make all our decisions within the boundaries of the factors that we cannot influence. These limitations include aspects such as biological influences; inter-personal relationships as well as the dynamics within our communities. It is virtually impossible to make any decision without the involvement of all of these factors in one way or the other. Thus, despite the lack of absolute autonomy, all of us, no matter how restrictive or disempowering the environment, have some form of decision autonomy when we make decisions, ranging from a high level to a low degree of decision autonomy.

Your decision autonomy is the level of influence you have in making a specific decision. There are two ways of looking at decision autonomy. The first is through the position you hold at school which allows you a specific remit to make decisions. On the other hand, you may have a personal preference for the level of decision autonomy: some people just don't like making decisions. For example, you may not be in a position of authority to make a decision, or you would rather prefer not to make a decision. Your decision autonomy is the most important aspect of how you make decisions in your life and no matter whether you have a high or low level of decision autonomy, this is the decision-making dimension that requires the most of your thinking.

Concerning your role at school, a high decision autonomy goes hand-in-hand with responsibility, accountability and expectations. For example, the principal of the school has very high decision autonomy, and a more junior leader has lower decision autonomy. Also, at school, you may have less decision autonomy than you have at home where you have a high level of decision autonomy. At home, your decisions involve your immediate family, and as suggested by game theory a steady series of compromises allow for a reasonably high level of autonomy. As a parent, inevitably with the responsibility of protecting and raising children the decision autonomy is much higher than that of a child. Conversely, you will not experience the same level of decision autonomy in the highly demarcated structures of the school.

On an individual level, your personality traits, emotional intelligence and confidence contribute significantly to the degree of decision autonomy you exert. You may find that extroverts exude a more significant deal of decision autonomy through their dominant personal qualities. However, the introvert's strong sense of self, clear personal boundaries and stated aspirations also contribute to having high decision autonomy.

You may have a low decision autonomy based on the remit of your role in school, however, there are also other social factors that determine a low decision autonomy. Gender, age, education level, religion, race all influence the degree of decision autonomy you hold. For example the discrimination against women in the workplace is still prevalent despite the fact that they are equally qualified. Women have the competence and capacity to make outstanding decisions, yet it is clear that they receive less decision autonomy. Race, continuously plays a role in people's freedom to make decisions despite the fact that there is no reason for such discrimination. We often find that younger leaders are given less freedom to choose despite their energy, skills and positive attitudes.

Because of these unfounded barriers, some people may lack the confidence to make individual decisions, thus placing them in the low decision autonomy part of the continuum. Self-determination theory suggests that a high level of autonomy makes us happier than a low degree of decision autonomy; however, it is worth remembering that high decision autonomy contributes more to elevated stress levels than having clear boundaries within which to make decisions.

Openness to Experience

Your personality plays an important role in the way you make decisions. Your *openness to experience* is linked with both seeking out new experiences and embracing unpredictability, which in turn, has a significant impact on the decisions you make. There are four factors that influence your openness to experience: your ability to process complex information; a sense of non-traditionalism, in other words, your tendency to have open-minded attitudes and progressive values; your curiosity and interest in exploring and understanding innovative ideas, and finally your ability to be introspective. In looking at how your openness to experience influences the way you make decisions, we place a *curious and inquisitive* approach on the one side of the continuum and a *cautious and careful* approach on the opposite side.

There are definite benefits and barriers to a cautious and careful approach to new experiences when making decisions. By being cautious and careful, you have the opportunity to reduce the level of risk that might be involved in your choices. It is beneficial to be watchful and aware of the consequences you may encounter when we make a choice. Also, when we do follow a cautious approach to decision-making, and we experience a positive result, it contributes to building a stronger self-esteem, and a positive self-esteem goes hand-in-hand with higher productivity, happiness and a healthy physical and social life. However, the opposite is also true. Cautious and careful decision-making may also leave you feeling a sense of discontent, increase procrastination to avoid making difficult decisions and even lead to learned helplessness. Conversely, you may have a curious and creative approach to new experiences.

Curiosity is defined as the recognition, pursuit, and intense desire to explore exciting, challenging, and uncertain events. Curiosity can also motivate people to act and think in new ways and investigate, be immersed, and learn about whatever is the immediate target of their attention. This definition captures the exploratory striving component and the mindful immersion component. By being curious, we do things for their own sake, and we are neither controlled by internal or external pressures that dictate what we should or should not do.

The relationship between curiosity and openness to experience is well documented and builds on an intellectual, reflexive and non-traditional approach to complex situations. Curiosity allows you to explore new and innovative approaches to existing problems without the bounded caution of the rule book. In the 21st Century, a sense of curiosity may very well be the driving force in an era where *new* is the keyword to humanity's very survival. However, throwing all experience and caution to the wind is never a good idea, and chasing novelty for the sake of the chase, over *tried-and-tested* methods, can lead to your teachers and students become tired and averse to constant change.

Control Patterns

Control patterns explore the amount of control and human agency we exercise over the decisions we make. Human agency is your innate capacity and need for, the freedom to control your behaviour. The *place* (or locus) where that control comes from is either internal or external. In other words your locus of control is your belief or perception about the cause of consequences in your life. If you have an external locus of control, you are very much influenced by stimuli within the environment, and you are *more passive and susceptible to external influence and cues*. If you have an internal locus of control, you depend on an internalised source of motivation based on your *perception of your work's significance, self-efficacy and your autonomy*. As with all the different approaches to decision-making, control patterns range on a spectrum from external/responsive control to internal/pro-active control.

An external/reactive control pattern is when you decide on a course of action in-the-moment or *on the spot*. External/ responsive control is precisely what the words suggest, an instantaneous response to something outside of you, without much reasoning or deliberation before you decide on a specific way to act. Some may argue that responsive control is not deciding at all, but rather an instinctive reaction. Some leaders have a preference for reactive decision-making, to rely on thinking on their feet, putting out the fires and on-the-spot decision-making.

Everyone has some idea of what it is they want, and through the course of time, we might even know more or less how we want to achieve it. However, an internal/proactive approach to decision-making depends on you having a clear set of goals, as well as having stated these goals in a clear and explicit way. You prefer to know what it is you want to achieve, and you like having a plan of action and a specific time frame in which to accomplish the goals.

Emotions

Emotions reflect a combination of conscious and un-conscious processes and behaviours. Emotions are consistently related to one another rather than discreet and independent. New research into the forming of emotions and how these feelings influence our actions, has been turning the world of psychology around. We now know that emotions are more than a mind *thing* and that a complex interplay between mind and body coincides to make us physically experience the emotions we feel. We also know that feelings are unique to individuals and that no other person can actually feel the emotions you feel. Your *happy* and my *happy* are entirely different despite the fact that we use the same word as a broad description of feeling happy.

The place where you think you are happy, the environment, your expectations and your previous experiences, concomitantly contribute in both a physical and mental way to create your very own, and exceptional feeling of happiness. Therefore, it stands to reason that the way in which your emotions influence your decision-making is utterly different than that of other people. Emotions can be seen in terms of activating, or deactivating (in other words emotions that inspire you to act, or make you want to do nothing).

In addition, emotions can either be pleasant or unpleasant. As an example, if you feel enthusiastic, your emotions can be seen as *activating and pleasant*, whereas, if you feel sad, we know this as *deactivating and unpleasant*. It makes sense that if your emotions have an enjoyable and activating impact on you, this will impact the decisions you make. Therefore, there are two ways that emotions influence decision-making. The first is by activating or deactivating you, and the second is how neutral or dependent you are on the activating or deactivating impact of emotions.

It is worth spending a few minutes considering the most prevalent emotion we have: fear. You can consider the role of fear as both an activating and deactivating emotion. Fear is hard-wired into your limbic system, specifically the amygdala, and it has an evolutionary survival function. Fear serves to protect us from risk, thus playing an empowering role in the decision-making process. It might be expedient to consider the importance of emotional states such as fear and doubt in the decision-making process as valuable guiding aspects of making effective decisions.

If you prefer to be emotion-neutral, under normal circum-stances, it does not imply that you are averse to emotions, nor does it suggest that being able to control your emotional state efficiently is more preferential that being dependent on your feelings when you make decisions. It is crucial for you to be self-aware of your emotions: emotional intelligence, a strong internal locus of control and a robust sense of human agency (intentionality, forethought, self-reactiveness and self-reflectiveness) form the crux of being emotion-neutral during the decision-making process. That being said, it is necessary to express that being emotion-neutral does not imply that your decisions will not hold up to moral scrutiny or will be inhumane. If your emotions play a significant part in how you make decisions, and you often feel the activating or deactivating effect of emotions, and if you are acutely aware of how your mood affects the light in which you view a specific problem or decision-making situation, you are emotion-dependent. However, this doesn't mean that because you are aware of your emotions that you experience decision-making paralysis – when you just cannot decide because how you feel. Most people can make a reasonably clear decision despite being aware of how they experience emotions at the time. However, when the deactivating effect of emotion dependence becomes an impending aspect during your decision-making process, we may consider this to be emotional noise.

Emotional noise is the niggling self-doubt that is burrowed in the back your head that insists on being heard, at full volume, once a decision needs to be made. This emotional noise is not part and parcel of a control pattern or personality type, but rather the emotions we have accepted either as a result of *many life lessons learned* or due to *in the moment experiences* such as shock or fear that have a debilitating impact on you.

Similarly, operational noise is a term that describes the everyday, routine decisions that are part-and-parcel of modern life: deciding which route will have least traffic problems and finding an outfit that fits and what to make for dinner tonight. These daily decisions do not need to take up all the decision-making energy we have, and often, these decisions are very much typical responsive decisions. However, when your stress levels continuously rise because of traffic, time pressure and inconsiderate bosses, then the operational noise can also become debilitating, having an additional negative impact on how you make choices.

Relative Decision-making Styles

Accepting the six characteristics of decision-making we explored previously. There are four relative decision-making styles: design/auditor, flexible, fluid and avoidant. The matrix in Figure 1 may help you understand how the six characteristics of decision-making contribute to your relative decision-making style. In the matrix, we place each of the opposing sides of the relevant components on a continuum. Follow the steps below to determine where you fall on the matrix.

Step 1: Think about each of the decision-making characteristics, and then decide where on the spectrum you feel most comfortable. Then indicate it on each of the continuums by making an x on the lines coded as AB, BC, CD and DA. On the reasoning and acuity lines, as well as the emotion and control pattern lines you find the average place between the two and indicate it with an x.

Step 2: Connect the x on lines AB with the x on CD with a straight line. Then connect the x on the BC line and the x on the DA line.

Step 3: Draw a small circle at the intersection where these connected lines cross.

Step 4: In the quadrant where you have drawn the small circle lies your relative decision-making style, which in turn indicates how you feel most comfortable in making decisions.

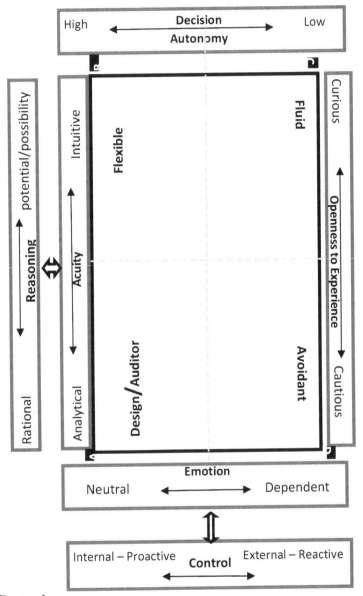

Figure 1:
Relative Decision-making Styles

Design/auditor

The design/auditor's reasoning is predominantly rational and this leader has a keen analytical acuity. On the decision autonomy continuum, the design/auditor perceives her freedom to make decisions as highly independent. In agreement with her reasoning style, the design/auditor's openness to experience leans towards being cautious. Her control patterns, depends on the locus of control is internal-proactive. Finally, the design/auditor is emotion-neutral in concordance with her rationality based reasoning style.

Characteristically, the design/auditor is a logical, plan-orientated decision maker. She considers the impact of any decision during a protracted research and preparation phase, and if all the consequences of a decision have not been evaluated, she would readily delay making a decision. The design/auditor can easily be accused of over-thinking a decision. The *design* aspect of this decision-making style is a significant distinguishing factor, of design/auditors. She will spend a substantial part of the decision-making process on designing a plan of action, which will include clear step-by-step instructions. The *"auditor"* aspect of the decision-making process means she insists on a high level of control and compliance. Every point of the decision-making process will be related to the plan.

Design/auditors are confident of the success of their decision as long as there are no unforeseen circumstances. Deviation from the plan causes a great deal of anxiety in the design/auditor because she has a distinct dislike of change. The design/auditor, as a leader, may favour a transactional leadership style where you follow a set plan and actions, rather than delegating decisions to the team.

237

Flexible

The flexible decision maker's reasoning style leans towards the potential/possibility end of the continuum. The flexible decision maker is highly aware that change is an inevitable part of process and she thrives on finding solutions to changing circumstance. On the decision autonomy continuum, the flexible decision maker has a high sense of autonomy. Her flexible decision-making style leans towards being curious and open to new experiences, which enables her to explore her intuition in searching for possible solutions to complex problems. Similar to the design/auditor, the flexible decision maker shows internal-proactive control patterns and is emotion-neutral in how she approaches a decision.

Characteristically, the flexible decision maker is goal orientated and will not refrain from changing plans to achieve the goal. She has a very clear understanding of what she wants the outcomes to look like, no matter how she reaches them. She believes that many roads lead to Rome and she will follow any and all avenues to the benefit of her teachers, students and support staff. She copes well with change and is firmly aware of the fluctuations in the environment, and she is good at adjusting accordingly. The flexible decision-making style may be most conducive to leaders that favour the transformational leadership style.

Fluid

In the same way as the flexible decision maker, a fluid style of decision-making shows a preference for potential/ possibility reasoning supported by a robust intuitive acuity. However, the fluid decision maker perceives herself to have low decision autonomy. She is curious in her openness to experience, and she shows partiality towards external-reactive control patterns. She is emotion-dependent when it comes to the activating and deactivating sways of her emotions, feelings and moods.

Characteristically, the fluid decision maker may experience anxiety when faced with a high-risk decision, and she would prefer to let others decide on her behalf. She prefers low conflict situations and will yield to pressure from opposing groups. The fluid decision maker may succumb to knee-jerk intuitive decisions that seem to be thoughtless and without reasoning.

She depends on the people around her, and she has a significant trust in her subconscious mind to come to the correct decision without much conscious consideration. The fluid decision maker as a leader may favour a laisser-faire style where she can delegate decision-making, based on their specific competencies and specialities, to empower members of her team.

Avoidant

The avoidant decision maker prefers a rational approach to making decisions and has an analytical acuity. However, the avoidant decision maker perceives herself to have low decision autonomy and is cautious in her openness to experience. She is responsive to outside stimuli in support of her external-reactive control patterns. She strongly depends on her emotions in making decisions.

Characteristically, the avoidant decision maker tends to make safe decisions based on democratic principles and consensus of the larger group. She may feel most comfortable to be a spectator, rather than a trailblazer such as flexible decision makers. She observes the possible pitfalls and risks associated with a specific decision and avoids making decisions as much as possible. There is a reason for the rulebook and she will follow every step diligently.

Avoidant decision makers often fall prey to procrastination and can become stressed and overwhelmed when tasks pile up due to indecision. Avoidant decision makers are wary of change and have a cautiously analytical stance towards implementing new policy and practice, but once the directive has come from above, she will not deviate from it.

The avoidant decision maker, as leader prefers to be a manager, and she favours a transactional leadership style where directives from above are unambiguous and non-negotiable.

Applied Leadership: How to use Relative Decision-making Styles

Firstly, one of the most significant characteristics of leadership is self-knowledge. In addition to having a clear understanding of your values, code of ethics and your moral imperative, knowing how you make decisions is one of the most influential tools you will have as a leader in education. This knowledge is convenient: for example, if you are a design/auditor you will know that one term's worth of planning is probably insufficient and that you will have to start your preparation much earlier in advance. If you have a flexible decision-making style, you will probably be frustrated and become distracted if the plan for the next academic year starts taking on form too early. The self-knowledge of your decision-making style also allows you to explore your areas for further professional development.

Exit Reflection

The majority of frustrations you will experience as a school leader will be related to how people make decisions. The teacher that is never on time with his grade progress report, the leader that makes knee-jerk decisions and the support staff member that refuses to take responsibility. All these *types* of people behave in specific ways because of the relative decision-making style. Having a clear understanding of why people behave in the way they do, is half the battle won, and allows you as their leader to address specific behaviours without feeling that those behaviours are deliberately contradictive to your vision or the expected teaching, learning and assessment behaviours. In the same way, for your teachers, students and support staff (even the school community at large) to have an understanding of your relative decision-making style can help them understand how to approach difficult discussions or problem situations with you. It allows them to avoid inappropriate or unnecessary conflict situations, which in turn allows for a better school climate.

Finally, students who have a clear understanding of their relative decision-making style can form a better understanding (especially during the tempestuous teenage years) of why and how they decide to do things. It could benefit them to understand how to develop their academic character and skills as well as navigate the stormy waters of teen friendships.

You should ask yourself:

☞ What is my decision-making style, and how does knowing how I make decisions help me empower my teachers and support staff?

☞ How does knowing the decision-making style of my leadership team, teachers and support staff help me to facilitate a culture and climate of care, diversity and high expectations?

X

MANAGING INTERPERSONAL CONFLICT IN THE WORKPLACE

Interpersonal conflicts in the workplace is a silent killer, especially in the school environment where a sense of psychological well-being needs to be maintained to achieve the best possible outcomes for the young people under your charge. You can expect a certain level of interpersonal conflict and disagreement in any setting, especially where a range of personalities are gathered. Such disagreements can even be seen as healthy, and if the general culture and climate of the school are right, such differences can also reinforce the school's drive for excellence. However, schools depend heavily on healthy inter-personal relationships to function well.

All human relationships serve to either satisfy our personal need for connection or not. This is an inevitability in interpersonal relationships. If you add the stresses of increasing expectations of personal accountability for ever-improving student outcomes; the different pedagogical approaches that have evolved between generations and the increased pressure brought about by changing technology, it is no wonder that the school environment has the potential to become a hotbed of interpersonal conflict.

Conflict can range from annoyances to clashes, to a crisis where disputes among your teachers reach a crisis point. Once you have entered such a crisis point, the differences between individuals can no longer contribute to a healthy dynamic culture and climate, but rather to stagnation. Work-related stress builds up and this leads to lowered productivity which in turn contributes to low levels of motivation. You, as the school leader, will play a significant role in preventing this downward spiral from happening, and if your school is already at such a crisis point, it is your duty to change the culture and climate of your school to.

Before we continue with understanding how to manage differences, we should remind ourselves what the difference between climate and culture in a school is. The culture of your school includes the typical daily interactions between teachers, support staff, students and parents. It also consists of the pedagogy, classroom and behaviour management strategies and what level of academic expectations you hold from students and faculty. The climate is a general feeling that you get when you enter the school. Climate has to do with emotions and general (almost intuitive) perceptions. The interpersonal relationships between all stakeholders in the school determine the culture and climate of the school, and how you manage differences plays a critical part in how these relationships develop. One of the responsibilities you will have is to manage and resolve a wide range of conflict situations on all levels. The truth of the matter is that it doesn't depend on your seniority whether you will be thrown into a raging torrent in a teacup. It is how you deal with conflict, that becomes your defining moment as a leader.

Conflict takes place on all levels and may include:

- conflict between local education authority and the governing body;
- conflict between governing body and principal;
- conflict between principal and leadership team;
- conflict among members of the leadership team;
- conflict between the leadership team and teaching and support staff;
- conflict between teachers and students;
- conflict among students of various minority groups;
- conflict between teachers and support staff;
- conflict among parent groups;
- conflict between teachers and parents;
- conflict between students and the neighbouring community;
- conflict between schools in the area.

When conflicts linger, they become crises, and the costs of an organisation in crisis is myriad. Firstly, the result of reaching a crisis point in the staff room results in the overall inefficiency of the school. Leaders make decisions based on the accurate and valid information they receive from various stakeholders. If the conflict between the different groups in the school has reached a crisis point, the validity and reliability of the information cannot be trusted, which in turn leads to decisions that are at best inefficient and at worst catastrophic. Two-thirds of performance problems in failing schools do not stem from a capability deficit of the staff, but rather because of ill-managed interpersonal relationships and its ensuing conflict.

Secondly, once conflict has reached a crisis point, you will soon lose skilled personnel. Good teachers can only become excellent teachers in a nurturing environment. However, if the school environment is toxic, your outstanding teachers will not find it difficult to move on to a school where the climate is much more positive. Losing excellent teachers will inevitably increase the workload of others, which increases stress levels, possible resentment and further conflict.

Thirdly, lowered motivation leads to ineffectual teaching and learning, the reduction value-added learning opportunities and a general lack of enthusiasm which is immediately felt by the students. If you don't resolve the conflict and the school climate does not improve, a lack of motivation quickly becomes a form of passive-aggressive resistance. Completing administrative duties late, failure to adequately implement and evaluate assessment opportunities and less than sufficient (if any) feedback to students further erodes the efficiency of the teaching and learning. At worst, some staff members may even go as far as full blown sabotage (which in the era of blogging and viral social media posts, has become one of the existential threats of any organisation). Finally, staff absenteeism because of stress-related health problems and increasing staff turnover has a direct influence on teaching and learning, resulting in ineffective student outcomes.

Emotion and Bias as Core Elements of Conflict

If we were to have the time to unpick every conflict situation, to find the core of the problem, we will find that at the heart of all interpersonal conflicts there are two main elements: emotion and bias. All behaviour is inseparable from emotions, and all emotions are inextricably linked to behaviour. Our behaviours are based on the expectations we hold about how the other person is going to respond to our actions and emotions. And expectations are based on our personal biases. In other words, that what we believe about ourselves and what we believe about others contribute, in a fundamental way, to how we feel and react in specific situations. Therefore, the emotions we experience during a conflict situation will add to the way we behave in response to the conflict.

Your self-serving bias is the tendency to take credit for success and avoid taking responsibility for failure. Self-serving bias is pervasive and has strong instinctive elements found in all human beings. It serves to protect us and our progeny from harm. Whether twenty thousand years ago, or right here and now in the modern world, we are surrounded by danger, and our fear and self-serving bias often serve as protecting forces against the threats we face. Therefore, we should not look at self-serving bias with disdain, but rather recognise that we are all prone to bias in our everyday decision-making. We should use this knowledge of our own biases to help us get to the root of why we feel what we feel.

There are three biases we hold when dealing with conflict situations: the *win-lose bias,* the *bad-person bias,* the *rock-in-the-road bias.* In the *win-lose bias*, you believe that there is no possible scenario where both parties can come out of a conflict situation as winners. You feel that either you are seen as the person that is correct or incorrect in a specific case. You may feel that you are not as dominant or persistent as the other person you will lose *the argument* and be seen as weak. It is this belief that a resolution to the conflict can only be binary and that a third way (*win-win*) cannot be an option that drives both parties to assert their power to be proven right. Quite often a simple conflict situation could have been resolved successfully, yet it has escalated to a crisis level because of the belief of both parties that if they don't *win* in the current conflict, they will come out with a damaged reputation or damaged authority. If you develop a culture in your school that provides the third option, where both parties can come out of the conflict in the *win* position, this immediately removes the perception that either party must fight to not be seen as the losing side.

Creating a culture of *win-win* starts with the choice of words that you generally in dealing with conflict. You can alleviate the impact of the win-lose bias when you use and demonstrate language that is socially inclusive. Inclusive language includes examples such as *"our" policies support creative problem solving, "together" we stand strong.* You should also emphasise promoting a cooperative stance *at "our" school, we all win when our students learn.* You also promote inclusive language when you replace personal ownership with collective ownership such as *our actions now make our students' future brighter.*

The *bad-person bias* asserts that the conflict is a result of one of the parties being incompetent, cruel, incapable and can only be resolved if one of the parties admits that they are of lesser capability. This bias depends on the Fundamental Attribution Error that there are people that are bad and others that are good. The *bad-person bias* is reciprocal and each person believes that the other is the *bad person*. In order to show that you are not incompetent, or incapable, cruel or stupid, your self-protection instincts force you to remain inflexible in the stance you take and thus allow no scope for resolution.

As the leader, you should create a school climate where teachers and staff have the scope to develop strengths and learn how to manage their areas of development. An open culture, where there is no fear of retribution because of an emerging skill; or a culture where your teachers are encouraged to discuss their areas for development, and are provided the opportunity to do training to develop these areas, removes the *bad-person bias* from a repertoire of conflict beliefs and behaviours.

The *rock-in-the-road bias* is based on the perception that differences are irreconcilable. This usually occurs after a protracted conflict situation has been allowed to simmer, and several attempts at resolution have failed. Both parties have concluded and maintain the belief that the differences are so significant and fundamental, that finding a solution is not possible. The difference between the *rock-in-the-road bias* and the other two biases is the sense of helplessness that comes as a result of the *rock* that blocks any way forward.

The insurmountable barrier to resolve a conflict is often as a result of a lack of conflict resolution skills on the side of leadership. If you ignore a conflict situation, there is a possibility that any barrier to creating a healthy school climate will become insurmountable. If you don't recognise the emotional impact conflict has on both parties, and if you don't address the feeling of fear on either side, you will face a ripple effect of dissent among the ranks. People will fear that they might experience financial, emotional or physical injury as a result of the conflict. If you do not implement effective conflict resolution strategies to create a school climate that is inclusive, accepting of differences, and has a pervasive feeling of unity and purpose, this *rock in your road,* will become insurmountable.

Removing the Elephant from the Room

Prevention is always better than cure and as far as conflict resolution in the school setting goes, this is every school leader's ideal. However, it would be unrealistic if you think that your teachers and support staff, leadership team and broader school community will never experience any form of conflict.

Disagreement and differences in opinion are part of education, as a matter of fact, learning is built on the premise that disagreement will occur and that through a rigorous process of debating and discussing fundamental issues, a form of truth will emerge that can be taught in the classroom. It is in this tradition of finding the truth, finding a better way of teaching, finding a more focused approach to ensure an inclusive environment, of finding the best support for every single child, that we admit that education is an industry where disagreement thrives. Creating a climate in which such disagreement is functional, respectful and seen in terms of a mutual vision – to improve the opportunities of every single child – is an essential part of preventing conflicts that turn into crises.

Create a Culture Conducive to Conflict Resolution

The first step to creating a culture conducive to inclusive attitudes and effective conflict resolution is to encourage open discussions about ideas and pedagogical beliefs. It is essential that teachers and support staff recognise their differences in approach, that they celebrate their diversity and believe that they can always get better at what they do. In establishing such a co-operative and open forum for discussion it is important to recognise other people's strengths, their experience, their knowledge, but also to make it clear that there are no *Tsars* in the school: everybody adheres to the mantra of *getting better never stops.*

Secondly, it is important to encourage open doors to specialists in their field. The inflexibility that becomes the fuel on the conflict fire is based on the need to protect oneself against embarrassment, retribution or losing a job. Therefore, reassuring staff that recognising their own areas for development will not lead to recrimination or disciplinary action, removes the instinctive self-protecting biases that encourages staff to hold onto their point of view for dear life.

Thirdly, you should be a role model and show your ability to recognise that your position is not the only right position. Show how to *listen to understand* the other person's point of view instead of listening in order to give a reply is the most powerful tool you have available. *If they see you practice, then you will not have to preach.* Discourage a culture of exclusivity, favouritism, and cliques. It is natural for groups that are similar minded to form, however, if you notice that these groups have taken on an air of exclusivity, soon gossip and favouritism will emerge, and if some teachers feel excluded from the rest, this is a sure way of establishing the foundation for conflict to turn into a crisis.

Finally, you should base the vision and ethos of the school on inclusivity, empathy and respect. If these values are modelled by the leadership team, they will soon take root in other areas of the school as well.

Despite all of the points mentioned above, there will come a time that all the *soft skills* in leadership will not be enough to extinguish the flames of conflict. At some point, you will have to take decisive steps to remove elements that thrive on discontent. Disciplinary action is never the first port of call; however, it is an option that is open to you, as leader, and one that should not be used as a threat, but rather through decisive action.

Find Time to Talk

Finding time to talk should not only be part of a formal conflict resolution strategy. Allowing teachers and support staff to share their ideas, beliefs, as well as their concerns on an interpersonal basis, allows a sense of camaraderie that may avert conflicts from even starting.

As part of a conflict management strategy, time should not become a barrier to solving problems. If two parties are finding themselves in a conflict situation that has spiralled to the point where mediation is needed, you must set time aside to find a sustainable solution. If this means that the two parties have to receive time off timetable, then it is worth paying for agency/supply teachers, or to organize an experiential learning day where the conflicting parties can spend time away from the buzz of the school day to find a resolution.

Conflict Resolution Skills

No matter how hard you have worked on creating a positive culture and climate in your team or school, there will come a time that conflict arises. Your instinctive reaction might be to let things resolve organically, however, such natural resolutions to conflict do not often happen easily. As a school leader, one of your defining skills will be how to resolve conflict situation.

Plan the Context

When dealing with a difficult situation you should have a clear plan according to which you aim to address pressing issues. Planning the context means that you lay out a set of *rules of mediation* that is agreed on before the resolution discussion takes place. You should discuss and decide on these ground rules individually. There must be a clear understanding that neither party can change these rules once the discussions have started. It is wise to include these *rules of mediation* in your school's staff handbook in the form of a Conflict Mediation Policy.

Aspects you should consider may include:

- agreed timeframe for mediation;
- agreed mediators;
- accepted choice of words (*we* rather that *you/I*);
- agreed reciprocal respect;
- agreement that the school vision and mission statements are the guidelines along which resolution is negotiated;
- statement of intent - *In this meeting it is my intention to;*
- accepted context of conflict, what is the actual problem;
- what will a win-win situation look like?
- what can be expected in terms of consequences if either party breaks the agreement?
- the role of personal representation during the discussion;
- personal representatives or union representation;
- the part union representation will play;

- who will take the minutes of the meeting and how will those minutes of the meeting be kept confidential?
- agreed confidentiality clauses that will prohibit either party to gossip .

Time and Place

The setting of mediation meetings is as important as the rules. If either party feels uncomfortable with where the meetings take place, the process is off to a less than favourable start. Once a neutral setting (not the principal's office) has been established, and the *rules of mediation* have been agreed, then the hard work starts. Some conflict resolution gurus suggest that there should be a time limit to discussions and that after a specific agreed time, the resolution process must be called to a halt and disciplinary action against both parties must be taken. I am ambivalent about how long it should take you to reach a mediation. However, I do agree that at some point you will reach an impasse where you have to agree to disagree, and you as the leader will implement further action according to the ethics code of the school to start disciplinary procedures.

Talk it Out

The mediator plays a critical part in establishing and maintaining the tone of the meetings. While talking it out, it is the mediator's responsibility to move the discussion forward in a fair, objective and unbiased manner. If you are the mediator, you may not choose side, and if such a situation is impossible, it is worth spending some money on employing a professional to become an impartial mediator for the situation. Most unions provide teachers and schools with ombudsman and legal services.

The tone of the meeting should be one of optimism, appreciation and respect. It is important to remind everybody that no matter how angry they get, it is worth asking for a moment's time out rather than storm out. Melodrama is least conducive of the possible behaviours and it is also often best to establish and maintain a sense of respect for the process rather than solve problems with humour.

The structure of the meeting may look as follows:

1. The opening – express appreciation for the willingness to participate in the mediation.
2. Express your optimism that a resolution will be found.
3. Remind both parties of the *rules of mediation.*
4. State the issue as you understand it. Come to an agreement about a concise problem statement that can be written down in a few words.
5. The invitation to participate. Agree who will state their point of view first, this should be done before the meeting starts.
6. The dialogue – stick to the issue at hand. Do not allow the discussion to wander off onto other topics, other people or expressing hopelessness.

Four principles for negotiating a *win-win* outcome will help you to have a more effective dialogue.

Separate the person from the problem. Do not resort to, or allow the conflicting parties to resort to the personal attributes of each other that may annoy. Emphasise the problem – this means that you may have to go back to the agreed problem statement.

Focus on the interest, not the positions. If you have managed to find a common interest that is important to both parties, it is easier to steer the discussion away from the divergent views they take. Often philosophical and pedagogical positions are so different that not the most skilled mediator can find common ground. However, in a school, it is much easier to find a common interest such as the progress of the students, which can form the fulcrum of the dialogue.

Invent options for mutual gain. Once you find a common interest, a more collaborate mood will allow you to become creative in finding a mutually beneficial agreement.

Identify objective criteria. Criteria to determine whether the mediation has been successful should be agreed upon as a final step before making a deal. The criteria must be objective, neutral, fair, legal, moral and in line with the school's vision.

Make a Deal

An agreement is only an agreement once it is on paper and signed in front of witnesses. Making the arrangement formal is an integral part of the mediation process. Both parties must understand that once they have entered into the mediation process, and they have engaged in the discussions to solve the conflict, there are only two options: *deal* or *no deal*. Both parties must know that they have to sign an agreement document in which you describe the expected behaviour and attitudes to make the agreement official. If they do not want to put pen to paper, the only alternative is *no deal* and this then opens them up to possible disciplinary action, or they could be placed under a formal *notice to improve*.

Notice to Improve

A *notice to improve* should be explained as part of the Professional Conduct Manual and agreement, a staff member must sign at the onset of his/her duties. If a teacher or support staff member is found to not hold the capability of fulfilling the job description; or their competency to provide effective teaching, learning and assessment opportunities; their conduct is not aligned with the school ethos or safeguarding policy; or other related duties, that teacher or support staff member can receive a *notice to improve*. The notice should stipulate the exact behaviour, expected measurable evidence to prove compliance and a time frame within which to develop.

Follow-up

Your aim with resolving the conflict is to establish a continued solution for both of parties' grievances. Setting a follow-up meeting to monitor the situation not only ensures both parties of your continuous support, but also provides them with the expectation that you are serious about the climate of cooperation you aim to establish in your school. Do not wait too long before the follow-up is scheduled. The first follow-up should be scheduled within two weeks of the mediation and then at least three more meetings with an increased timespan between each that follow.

The follow-up meeting should not be one that is neglected in terms of time and effort, but rather show clear commitment to the *win-win* solutions that were found. The worst thing you could do is to forget about follow up or, in the rapid pace of school leadership postpone the follow up meeting. If you show through your own behaviour that the mediation process is not important enough, your teachers and staff will not take it seriously either. The second aspect of a follow up meeting should include is a discussion about *what went well* and *even better if*. You can expect that not everything has been smooth sailing and that frustrations will most certainly have occurred. These must be openly discussed and solutions found before the frustrations turn into conflict or a crisis.

Limitations to Resolving Conflict

Not all conflict resolutions will be equally successful. As your experience grows, you will develop a sense of what works and what to avoid doing again. There are several aspects that should not be part of your conflict resolution menu.

Do not ignore the problem. Conflicts never resolve themselves. In the school setting, it is a near guarantee that an unresolved conflict will have a further reaching deleterious impact. The head-in-the-sand approach will always mean that you have to address the problem when it is inevitably more difficult to solve.

Do not use power plays. Threatening your staff with actual or possible disciplinary action shows a weakness in managing the interpersonal relationships in your school, and both teachers and students can *smell fear.* Your inability to constructively address conflicts on any level of the school opens up the perception with all stakeholders that you do not have the capacity for ethical leadership that will protect them when it is most needed.

Do not withdraw and start ignoring your staff. Such tactics are not constructive, and taking on a passive-aggressive stance towards the conflicting parties will not resolve their crisis, nor will it stop the spread of further conflicting situation in your school.

Check your language, check their language. There should be a firm stance against the use of inflammatory language, derogatory terms, personal insults, name-calling, and most certainly no discriminatory racial, gender or orientation-based language.

Stay alert. When you are mediating a conflict, there is nothing worse than starting to think about the rest of your day and how much you resent the conflicting parties for not being able to work together. Conflict resolution is not a waste of time; it is a step towards creating an open and inclusive school.

Listen to understand, not to reply. Your biggest strengths as mediator are to listen with empathy, beyond the emotions that are tinting the moment, and in such a way as to understand the actual problem beyond the superficial conflict. If anything, it is your job to reflect the facts as you hear them back to the two parties, rather than make an interpretation of what their conflict means.

Do not judge. A mediation session is not a tribunal. You are very far away from anybody having to judge the merits of any conflict situation, and therefore it is not wise to place yourself in the position of judge and jury, even if you feel like you want to point out who you think is correct. It is not within your remit to make a character judgement or take sides. You are in a position of complete impartiality, and if the circumstance is such that you do not have the skill set to be impartial, or the matter at hand is such that you find yourself leaning towards any one of the two parties, it is worth the time and money to find fair and independent mediators to assist.

Do not become frustrated. Time is the most valuable asset we all have. It is worth every penny and pound to invest in a successful conflict resolution. Do not rush the process, do not become frustrated and do not show your anger at any one of the parties if they are slow to concede their position. And if you are frustrated, don't show it. Remember the outcome of the mediation is a *win-win* solution and until both parties do not feel that this is the case, your job is not yet done.

Do not take a failed mediation as personal. A failed intervention is an opportunity for you to reflect and learn. What went ok? Why did things go so well and then suddenly anger flared up again? How can you improve on making both parties feel safe – at the same time? There will be times that you will have to concede that the mediation did not work and that you will need professional help to manage the crisis. Finding professional support is not a personal slant against you, your leadership style or your capability. You might initiate a mediation session and realise that the one point, the two parties agree on is that they don't want you to be the mediator. This too is not personal. They may just feel that they should not air certain parts of their dirty laundry in front of a leader who also gets to decide their next performance bonus. Respect their choice and find a different mediator.

The Psychology of Turning Conflict into Cooperation

The first lesson we learn from psychology is that the problem doesn't have to be solved for the conflict to be resolved. Conflict originates from emotions, biases and perceived injustices. Anger, resentment, fear and animosity are all emotions that people feel during a conflict situation. The conflict itself is not started by a problem, but rather by the perceptions each of the disagreeing parties hold regarding the problem. These perceptions are fuelled by the innate a well as the learned biases that are typical to each one of us. Thus, when resolving the conflict, it is not the actual problem that we are addressing, it is the interpersonal and intrapersonal psychological aspects that causes and sustains the conflict, that needs to be addressed.

You may feel ill-equipped to deal with people's emotions, not only because emotions are so very personal, but also because your intrapersonal world may be as messy everybody else's. The fact is that unpleasant emotions such as anger and animosity are part of everyday life, and having a forum in which to express that anger, in a trusting environment, is not as scary and self-revealing as you may think. Allowing them to express their anger and disappointment allows each of the parties to identify with the emotions they feel and recognise that they have the anger that is aroused during the conflict in common and that it feels better for them to not be angry. Thus, the aim of the mediation is not to find the bolts and nut solution to the problem, but rather to cultivate respect for different opinions and viewpoints; the enhancement of mutual trust; the acceptance of differences and to recognise that a two-fold rope is stronger than one rope at a time. The emotional impact the mediation may have on you is also an important aspect to consider.

Leadership, at the best of times, is not the most social of activities – feeling isolated and even lonely is often reported by leaders that have been in the game for some time. The fact that the mediation is conducted in confidence places a compelling responsibility on you to not divulge what was expressed during the meeting. In the same way, during the negotiation expressed emotions or positions, may be closer to home than you anticipate.

You may very well identify with or even agree with one of the parties, and because you are not permitted to choose a side or show your point of view, it can leave you feeling angry and more isolated. You may experience that some of the talking points raised during the discussion invoke memories of similar unpleasant experiences you have had, which in turn could arouse deeper feelings of resentment and unresolved issues of trust.

Finally, the role of personality factors may play a significant role in the reason why the two parties have started to disagree. To direct the mediation away from emphasising aspects that neither side can change in a single meeting (personality factors are relatively stable, and even though personalities can adjust over time, they rarely make leaps and bounds in the span of an afternoon's mediation session).

There are eight prerequisites to ensure that the mediation can actually be successful and that a different approach would not be more useful. 1) the conflict must be a two-person conflict. Where there are three or more divergent views, opinions and beliefs a different resolution strategy is needed, and you would be best advised to contact a professional group therapist to help you with this. 2) The two people have an ongoing, interdependent relationship. It is not worth trying to solve the conflict between a delivery man that has visited the school site once or twice and the security guard. Just ask for another delivery man and retrain the security guard. 3) Both people are present and involved in the dialogue. If one of the parties withholds or withdraws from the discussion, you cannot come to a resolution. As stated earlier, the conflict situation may remind one of the sides of hurtful childhood memories and they may have learned that remaining emotionally distant from others is the best form of self-preservation. In this case, you should have a serious discussion with this person about seeing a professional counsellor help him resolve intrapersonal conflict which may very well be the antecedent to the interpersonal conflict he is experiencing. 4) Each person must be able to refrain from physical violence and restrain impulsive behaviours. Health and safety cannot be compromised, and if one of the parties is incapable of self-control, you should aim to find an alternative solution through a professional mediator. 5) Power is not severely imbalanced, and neither person characteristically abuses power. Trying to find resolution when either of the two parties show narcissistic personality factors is a waste of time. Power, control games and dishonesty are characteristics of a narcissist, and the three things that will arrest progress in mediation are power, control games and deception. 6) Neither person is addicted to chemical substances. The dependence on chemical substances renders an addict incapable of the empathy and self-control that is needed when finding a *win-win* resolution to a conflict. As a matter of fact, the antecedent to the conflict may be the addition and subsequent related irrational and uncontrolled behaviours and emotions. 7) Neither person suffers from severe emotional disorders. Again, if one of the parties has a mental health disorder, it is best left to the professionals to address the dysfunction first before attempting any form of reconciliation and finally, 8) Both speak the same language. Miscommunication is often the root of the conflict, and where there is an inability to communicate, including complicated emotions, the resolution will not be successful.

For both the mediator as well as the two parties there is an uncomfortable truth, and that is that to have a successful resolution all parties will have to be accepting of discomfort. The fact is conflict is unpleasant, and despite the discomfort, an imperfect resolution may hold, it is much less painful than the continuous stress of an ongoing dispute.

Mental Health Awareness in the Workplace

Personality disorders and other mental health disorders such as post-traumatic stress disorder, bi-polar disorder and substance abuse are all very real problems people face in the workplace. A significant number of teachers are diagnosed with mental health disorders, and the fact that they still function well notwithstanding their mental health difficulties, their mental health difficulties renders it near impossible to become outstanding education practitioners.

These disorders also often have a critical impact on the interpersonal relationships with colleagues. If you suspect that any of your teachers or staff members suffer from a mental health disorder it is worth the time and effort to invest in an awareness campaign to help staff find the appropriate support they need.

It is important to consider what the person without the personality disorder, mental health difficulties or additional problems can do about the conflict? The answer is not very much. In such a case where the cognitive ability or other mental health issue come into play, these will render any attempt at mediation ineffective. They could wait until they have resolved the underlying mental health difficulties, but this may take a very long time or not ever happen. This is where the more rational and emotionally healthy party takes a deep breath, accepts that not all conflicts can be solved, and move on. It would be wise for teachers with mental health difficulties to find a counsellor herself and discuss the anger, resentment and abhorrence she experienced during the conflict. This could help them, and you, grow and become stronger to face another day.

Exit Reflection

Conflict in the staffroom is a double-edged sword. It can inspire teachers to reach for new heights in their TLA, it can motivate them to go that extra mile, and it can lead to enthusiastic conversations about the nature of learning and the future of education. But conflict can also have a paralysing effect, leading to disengagement, toxic cliques and a disaffected workforce. Managing the school's climate and culture in such a way that conflict can become a force for growth rather than stagnation is no mean feat. To add to the uncertainty of working with interpersonal conflict in the staffroom, there is no sure way of ensuring that the motivational strategies, standard operating procedures and your attempts at establishing an inclusive culture in your school will always be successful. As a school leader your will need to grow a thick skin, you will have to develop the courage to have the difficult conversations that are needed from time to time and the conviction that your purpose in changing lives is unwavering.

XI

COMMUNICATION, COMMUNICATION, COMMUNICATION

Communication is one of the most important aspects of your leadership development. Whether it is one-on-one communication between you and a teacher, your ability to address groups, compose a clear and concise e-mail message or express your vision for the future compelling, persuasive and clear communication forms part of everything you do. It is also your role as leader to be the ambassador for your school in the broader community, and this encompasses a more extensive set of skills than clarity, conciseness and persuasiveness. In addition to these skills, you will also have to develop a clear and compelling communications plan as a roadmap for how you will keep all the stakeholders of the school informed and connected with your vision.

The Communication Plan

The communications plan might focus on the goals you have set out for the school or your department, or it might guide the marketing and reputation building of the school's brand. There are no definitive rules of guidelines for communications planning of a school. You may want to address the following points to help you design your communications plan:

- ✎ **Time span.** Trying to communicate a large number of priority points at once will make your communication hazy and leave the audience unsure of what you want them to know. Whether you wish to inform stakeholders of significant changes in practice or the vision of the school or ongoing communication of relevant information, it is essential to divide the period over which you wish to communicate your message into regularly scheduled time slots. Not only does this create an expectation with stakeholders that they will receive necessary information, but it also helps you plan your communications strategy, budgetary requirements and time for branding and design over the medium term.

- ✎ **Goals.** It is important that the message you want to share should be directly linked to your vision, goals and strategies. Answers to, why it is important to communicate during the envisaged time period? What do you want to achieve through the communications and what are the top one or two priorities you consider most important to communicate, will help you decide how, where, when and through which medium you will communicate?

🏵 **Strategies.** Depending on the goals that you have set, you will be able to judge of the message you wish to communicate can be reduced to a brief burst of communication or whether something of more substance is needed to ensure clarity and comprehension. It is worth noting that if your message is long, complicated and requires a great effort to write, it will be difficult to read and understand. You should probably return to the specific reasons you need to communicate the information as well as to consider whether you are not trying to share too much information in one message. Depending on the content of your message, you can think about the specific ways in which you hope to reach your goals, connect with your audiences, share information, and receive feedback. These strategies could include newsletters, short message push notifications (sending group SMS messages) headlines on the school's website or push notifications on the school's student management system. If you are making use of a social media account to communicate with stakeholders, you may want to include images to attract attention on the dashboard or news feed.

🏵 **Audiences.** There are various groups within your school community that you will have to reach any point in time. Some messages may only be for teachers, and some for all staff. Some messages may be focused on students that are of specific age or part of a particular focus group; you may wish to attract the attention of the school community or the broader community to establish a positive reputation or change the community's perceptions of the school. It is vitally important that you carefully consider what it is you want to communicate and with whom. If you misjudge your audience, their perceptions, needs and views of your school, the damage to your school's reputation could take a very long time to rectify, if ever. It may cost a significant amount of money to repair.

✶ **Key messages.** Communication is never as simple as getting a single piece of information to a specific audience. There are always sub-texts, perceived meaning, biases and branding implications that you need to keep in mind. Placing exam dates in the local newspaper may communicate to some that you are conscientious and want to ensure that all stake-holders are aware of these critical days, but to others, it may indicate that you don't have a solid internal communication strategy and that you are covering all the bases to protect yourself. Publicising the success of a top achieving student in the local media may indicate to some that you are celebrating the success of your students, and to others, it may mean that you are elitist and that the attention students receive are limited to the wealthy and high attaining students only. There are no fool-proof ways of ensuring that your audience's individual biases don't shade the message you aim to communicate, however, you may have a policy of celebrating achievement through placing pictures of a diverse group of students in the newspaper. You may decide to celebrate progress over time rather than highest grade. Or include the community service of some students alongside the academic achievement of others.

✶ **Responsibilities.** The what, the where, the when, the why and the how of communication are aspects that you should carefully consider. Also, the quality and accuracy of press releases, the choice of vocabulary, quality of images, diversity of students in these pictures, and the consistency of brand imaging, and most of all the correct use of language and spelling are all aspects that must be consistent over time. It is best advised that one person has the responsibility and authority to take lead of the communications policy and plan, rather than have a shoot-from-the-hip approach to getting a picture in the newspaper.

🔖 **Timelines.** You must know when things need to happen, the process of procurement of advertising, or getting into the community pages, the process of getting authorisation to use instant messaging as a communication tool as well as quality assurance strategies such as having the languages depart-ments check for clarity and accuracy. It is never wise to rush an e-mail, instant message or post on social media without having several people review the text. This process takes time, and it is, therefore, wise to make sure that you are ahead of the ball-game, rather than reactive.

It is essential to review your communication plan regularly and evaluate the effectiveness of your strategies. It is worth it to ask members of the school community, in person or through brief surveys, whether they feel that information sharing is appropriate, clear and taking place at acceptable intervals. It is also crucial that you ensure that the media you choose to use as your primary form of communication is accessible to your primary audience.

Social Media

Twitter, Facebook, YouTube, Pinterest, Tumblr, Snapchat and Rate My Teacher (RMT), to name but a few, are everywhere. And as soon as you think you have caught on to what the newest

Exit Reflection

Successful communication is based on your appreciation of the process, the audience, the intent and the content of what you want to communicate. In addition, your ability to listen beyond emotions, to listen past assumptions and to listen despite your innate self-serving bias is a crucial aspect of being an effective communicator. If you fail in effective communication, your leadership will not reach the level of mastery that you are capable of reaching.

You should ask yourself:

- Am I clear about the whole idea , do I know what the big picture is and what the details are that I want to communicate?
- Have I met the communication needs and interests of my audience? Am I using the correct medium and am I communicating what they need to hear in a way that can understand?
- Have I asked somebody to check and double check the clarity, conciseness and consistency of my communication? Did I communicate what I think I communicated?
- Is my tone, level of language, and content accessible for my audience?
- Is there a clear "call to action" ? Did I include clear and correct next steps in my communication?
- Have I been inclusive and respectful of diversity in my style, tone and language?

Dr Jacques Mostert

XII

Finally

I started this book by placing emphasis on the fact that you have embarked on a voyage of change. One in which the way you look at yourself should not remain the same by the end of it. I warned that the journey is deeply personal, often unfair and usually very lonely. If you have reached this part of the book, and I suspect not many who have started to read it have, you have either paged to the back to see how it ends (like my dear friend and mentor Nadia always does) or you have emerged as a completely different person.

I do not claim to have some sage words that will be the cornerstone of your continuous journey from here on. But I do know that what you are doing as a school leader, is purposeful and does contribute to making lives better one child at a time. I do want to leave you with the wisdom of Lucy Giles:

"Life is about doing the right thing, on a difficult day, when no one is looking"

Dr Jacques Mostert

INDEX

Bibliography

Begley, P. T., & Johannson, O. (2003). *THE ETHICAL DIMENSIONS OF SCHOOL LEADERSHIP* (Vol. 1). Dordrecht: KLUWER ACADEMIC PUBLISHERS.

Booth, T., & Ainscow, M. (2011). *Index for Inclusion: Developing Learning and Participation in Schools.* (3rd ed.). England: Centre For Studies on Inclusive Education.

Brennan, R. (2014). Reflecting on Experiential Leaning in Marketing Education. *The Marketing Review,* 97-108.

Buttris, J., & Callender, A. (2008). *A-Z Learning Diifculties and Disabilities* (2nd ed.). Cambridge, UK: Optimus Publications.

Capowski, G. (1994, March). Anatomy of a Leader: Where are the Leaders of Tommorow? *Management review, 83*(3), 12.

Clemens, M. D., & Cord, B. A. (2013). Assessment Guiding Learning: Developing Graduate Qualities in an Experiential Learning Programme. *Assessment & Evaluation in Higher Education, 38*(1), 114-124.

Connoly, B. S., Ones, D. S., & Chernyshenko, O. S. (2014). Introducing the Special Section on Openness to Experience:Review of Openness Taxonomies, Measurement, and Nomological Net. *Journal of Personality Assessment,* *96*(1), 1–16. doi:10.1080/00223891.2013.830620

Cornell, R. M., Johnson, C. B., & Schwartz, W. C. (2013). Enhancing Student Experiential Learning with Structured Interviews. *Journal of Education for Business, 88*, 136-146.

Department for Education. (2014). *Special Education Needs and Disability Code of Practice: 0-25 years.* United Kingdom: Government Published.

Department of Basic Education Republic of South Africa. (2017). *National Curriculum Statements (NCS) Grades R - 12.* Retrieved September 18, 2017, from Department of Basic Education Republic of South Africa: https://www.education.gov.za/Curriculum/NationalCurri culumStatementsGradesR-12.aspx

Dutta, R. (2014). A Case for Inclusion: visually impaired learners. *SEN Magazine.*

Ernst, J. V. (2013). Impact of Experiential Learnig on Cognitive Outcome in technology and Engineering Teaching Preparation. *Journal of technology Education., 24*(2), 31-40.

Feldman- Barret, L., Niedenthal, P. M., & Winkielman, P. (2005). *Emotion and Consiousness.* New York: The Guilford Press.

Haddon, M., & Stephens, S. (2016). *The Curious Incident of the Dog in the Night-Time.* (M. Elliot, Director, & N. Cusack, Performer) Apollo Theatre, Shaftsbury Avenue, London, United Kingdom.

Homburg , C., & Prigge, J.-K. (2014). Exploring Subsidiary Desire for Autonomy: A Conceptual Framework and Empirical Findings. *Journal o f International Marketing, 22*(4), 21-43.

Joffe, H. (2017, September 20). World Bank:lack of innovation stifles SA. (H. Joffe, Ed.) *Business Day*, p. 1.

Johnson, M. (2007). Chapter 3: "Where are we now: 1976 and all that". In *Subject to Change: New Thinking on the Curriculum* (pp. 40-62). UK: The Green Tree Press.

Kahneman, D., & Tversky, A. (2000). *Choices, Values and Frames.* Cambridge: Cambridge University Press.

Kahneman, D., & Tversky, A. (2000). *Choices, Values, and Frames.* Cambridge, UK: Cambridge University Press.

Karten, T. (2010). *18 Inclusion Strategies for Student Success.* Retrieved September 26, 2017, from Teachhub.com: http://www.teachhub.com/18-inclusion-strategies-student-success

Karwowski, M. (2012). Did Curiosity Kill the Cat? Relationship Between Trait Curiosity, Creative Self-Efficacy and Creative Personal Identity. *Europe's Journal of Psychology, 8*(4), 547–558. doi:10.5964/ejop.v8i4.513

Kashdan, T. B. (2009). The curiosity and exploration inventory-II: Development, factor structure, and psychometrics. *Journal of Research in Personality.,* 987-998. doi:10.1016/j.jrp.2009.04.011

Kedia, B. L., & Nordtveldt, R. (2002). International Business Strategies, Decision Making Theories, and Leadership Styles: an INtegrative Framework. *Competitive Review, 12*, 38-52.

Leithwood, K., & Seashore-Louis, K. (2012). *"Linking Leadership to Student Learning"*. San Francisco: John Wiley & Sons.

Li, Y., Wei, F., Ren, S., & Di, Y. (2015). Locus of control, psychological empowerment and intrinsic motivation relation to performance. *Journal of Managerial Psychology, 30*(4), 422-438. doi:http://dx.doi.org/10.1108/JMP-10-2012-0318

Lin, C.-C., & Lin, G. T. (2014, July). ANALYZING INNOVATION POLICY DIMENSIONS AND CONTEXTS: IN THE EMPIRICAL CASES OF TAIWAN AND SINGAPORE. *International Journal of Organizational Innovation, 6*(4), 114-128.

Long, M., Wood, C., Littleton, K., Passenger, T., & Sheehy, K. (2011). *The Psychology of Education* (2nd ed.). London: Routledge.

Long, M., Wood, C., Littleton, K., Passenger, T., & Sheehy, K. (2011). *Yhe Psychology of Education* (2nd ed.). London: Routledge.

Lord, R. G., & Dinh, J. (2014, June). What Have We Learned That Is Critical in Understanding Leadership Perceptions and Leader-Performance Relations? *Industrial & Organizational Psychology., 7*(2), 158-177. doi:10.1111/iops.12127

Malewska, K. (2015). Intuition in Decision Making -Theoretical and Empirical Aspects. *International Journal of Business & Economic Development., 3*(3), 97-105.

Marques, J. (2015). The Changed Leadership Landscape: What Matters Today? *Journal of Management Development, 34*(10), 1312.

Meyer, H. W. (2005, January). *The nature of information, and the effective use of information in rural development.* (D. o. Science, Producer, & University of South Africa) Retrieved November 8, 2017, from Information Research: http://www.informationr.net/ir/10-2/paper214.html

Ministry of Education - New Zealand . (2012). *Leading from the Middle.* Professional Leadership: Schooling Group. Learning Media Limited.

Mitchell, P., & Ziegler, F. (2013). *Fundamentals of Developmental Psychology.* (Second Edition ed.). New York: Psychology Press.

Morris, L. (2013). Three Dimensions of Innovation. *International Management Review, 9*(2), 5-10.

Mosthekga, A. (2011). Economic and Management Sciences. *Curriculum and Assessment Policy Statement.* Pretoria, Gauteng, South Africa: Department of Basic Education. Retrieved from National Curriculum Statement (NCS).

Niedenthal, P. M., Barsalou, L. W., Ric, F., & Krauth-Gruber, S. (2005). Embodiment in the Acquisition and Use of Emotion Knowledge. In L. Feldman-Barret, P. M. Niedenthal, & P. Winkielman (Eds.), *Emotion and Consciousness* (p. 23). New York: The Guilford Press.

OECD. (2015). *Measuring R&D Tax Incentives*. Retrieved August 18, 2016

OECD. (2015). *OECD Data and Statistics on R&D Tax Incentives*. Retrieved August 18, 2016, from http://www.oecd.org/sti/RDTaxIncentives-Data-Statistics-Scoreboard.pdf

Office of National Statistics. (2005). *Mental health of children and young people in Great Britain: A Case for Autistic Learners*. Office of National Statistics. London: Palgrave Macmillan.

Petri, H. L., & Govern, J. M. (2013). *Motivation: Theory, Research and Application* (6th ed.). USA: Wadsworth, Cengage Learning.

Pierangelo, R., & Giuliani, G. J. (2007). *The Educator's Diagnostic Manual of Disabilities and Disorders*. San Francisco, CA: John Wiley & Sons.

Pillay, J., Dunbar-Krige, H., & Mostert, J. (2013). Learners with behavioural, emotional and social difficulties' experiences of reintegration into mainstream education. *Emotional and Behavioural Difficulties., 18*(3).

Rehman, R. R., & Waheed, A. (2012). Individual's Leadership and Decision Making Styles: A Study of Banking Sector of Pakistan. *Journal of Behavioural Sciences , 22*(3), 70-89.

Rehman, R. R., & Waheed, A. (2012a). Transformational Leadership Style as Predictor of Decision Making Styles: Moderating Role of Emotional Intelligence. *Pakistan Journal of Commercial Social Sciences, 6*(2), 257-268.

Rehman, R. R., & Waheed, A. (2012b). Individual's Leadership and

Decision Making Styles: A Study of Banking Sector of Pakistan. *Journal of Behavioural Sciences, 22*(3), 70-89.

SCCD. (n.d.). *Inclusive Education and SEN: From Warnock to Present*. Schools Courses & Career Development.

Scott, S. G., & Bruce, R. A. (1995). Decision-Making Style: The Development and Assessment of a New Measure. *Educational and Psychological Measurement, 55*, 818-831.

Simon, H. A. (1997). *Administrative Behavior: A Study of Decision-making Processes in Administrative Organization*. (4th ed.). New York, NY: Free Press.

Solansky, S. T. (2014). To Fear Foolishness for the Sake of Wisdom: A Message to Leaders. *Journal of Business Ethics, 122*, 39-51.

Spicer, D. P., & Sadler-Smith, E. (2005). An Examination of the General Decision Making Style Questionnaire in Two UK Examples. *Journal of Managerial Psychology, 20*(2), 137-149.

Szatmari, P. (2011). What are ASC? In S. Bölte, & J. Hallmayer (Eds.), *Autism Spectrum Disorders: FAQs on Autism, Asperger Syndrome, and Atypical Autism answered by International Experts*. (pp. 1-7). Cambridge, MA: Hogrefe Publishing.

Tacy, P. (2006). *Ideals at Work: Education for World Stewrdship in the Round Square Schools*. Massachusettes: Deerfield Academy Press.

Together we learn better:Inclusive Schools Benefit All Children. (2015). *Inclusive Schools*, pp. 66-68.

Tripathi, M. N. (2015). Dissecting Affect : An Attempt to Understand its Influence on. *Vilakshan: The XIMB Journal of Management, 12*(1), 97-114.

Tversky, A., & Fox, C. R. (2000). Weighing Risk and Uncertainty. In D. Kahneman, & A. Tversky (Eds.), *Choices, Values, and Frames* (pp. 93-117). Cambridge: Cambridge University Press.

Useem, M. (2010). Decision Making as Leadership Foundation. In N. Nohria, & R. Khurana (Eds.), *Handbook of Leasdership Theory and Practice: A Harvard Business School Centennial Colloquium.* Boston, USA: Harvard Business School Publishing Corporation.

Vogel, K. (2016, January 4). *5 Effective Strategies for the Inclusive Classroom.* Retrieved September 26, 2017, from KQED Education: https://ww2.kqed.org/education/2016/01/04/5-effective-strategies-for-the-inclusive-classroom/

Vroom, V. H. (2000). Leadership and the Decision-making Process. *Organizational Dynamics, 28*(4), 82.

Yin, R. K. (2013). *Case Study Research: Design and Methods* (5th Edition ed.). Sage Publications.

Yulk, G. (2012, November). Effective Leadership Behavior: What We Know and What Needs More attention? *Academy of Management Perspectives, 26*(4), 68. doi:10.5465/amp.2012.0088

www.iale.org.za

Printed in Great Britain
by Amazon